U.S. Fish & Wildlife Service

2011 Annual Report
Migratory Bird
Conservation Commission

Table of Contents

The Service's Legacy of Conserving Migratory Waterfowl Habitat

For more than 80 years, the Federal Duck Stamp Program and Migratory Bird Conservation Program have helped secure key habitats to sustain migratory bird populations. They protect wetlands, help dissipate storm runoff, purify water supplies, and store flood water. As we look forward to the future conservation of these critical resources, we can find inspiration in these programs' extraordinary history of success.

PINTAIL

At the turn of the 20th century, overeager hunters and the commercial demand for meat and feathers had decimated waterfowl populations. At the same time, periodic droughts caused wetlands and other valuable waterfowl habitat to disappear. In the late 1920s, conservationists, hunters, and government officials worked together to create the Migratory Bird Conservation Act, which Congress passed in 1929. This landmark legislation authorized the Federal government to acquire and permanently protect wetlands for waterfowl. It also created the Migratory Bird Conservation Commission—composed of Federal and State officials—to consider and approve proposals for land acquisition.

Although the Act gave the government authority to create migratory bird refuges, it did not provide a permanent source of acquisition funding. This problem was addressed in the 1930s when President Franklin D. Roosevelt appointed Jay N. "Ding" Darling, a nationally known wildlife conservationist and political cartoonist, to serve as the Chief of the Bureau of Biological Survey. Darling was instrumental in the creation of a stamp, to be purchased by all waterfowl hunters, that would generate funds to pay for the acquisition of waterfowl habitat. In 1934, Congress passed the Migratory Bird Hunting and Conservation Stamp Act, which required all hunters older than 16 to purchase and possess a Federal Duck Stamp while hunting waterfowl. Revenues from Duck Stamp sales are now deposited in the Migratory Bird Conservation Fund. The fund also includes import duties collected on arms and ammunition, receipts from permits for rights-of-way across refuge lands, and any appropriations from the Wetlands Loan Act, which Congress authorized in 1961 as an advance of funds against future revenues from sale of Duck Stamps.

Since 1934, the Service has spent more than $1 billion Migratory Bird Conservation Fund dollars to permanently protect more than five million acres of important waterfowl habitat—including nearly three million acres of waterfowl production areas in the U.S. Prairie Pothole Region. In 2011 alone, the Service used almost than $34 million in funds from the Migratory Bird Conservation Fund to purchase, lease, or protect via easement nearly 30,000 acres of waterfowl habitat at migratory bird refuges and almost 22,000 acres in the Prairie Pothole Region.

Today as in the past, the Federal Duck Stamp Program and Migratory Bird Conservation Program depend on the support of people who understand and connect with our natural world—people who understand the importance of our wildlife resources and take action. What can you do? Buy a Federal Duck Stamp. Tell people how important Federal Duck Stamps are to ensuring healthy populations of all migratory birds and other wildlife. For more information, visit our Federal Duck Stamp Web site <www.fws.gov/duckstamps> or our Division of Realty Web site <www.fws.gov/refuges/realty>.

The Migratory Bird Conservation Commission

Section 2 of the Migratory Bird Conservation Act of 1929 established the Migratory Bird Conservation Commission. It reads as follows:

Section 2, as amended. A Commission to be known as the Migratory Bird Conservation Commission, consisting of the Secretary of the Interior, as Chairman; the Administrator of the Environmental Protection Agency; the Secretary of Agriculture; two Members of the Senate, to be selected by the President of the Senate; and two Members of the House of Representatives, to be selected by the Speaker, is created and authorized to consider and pass upon any area of land, water, or land and water that may be recommended by the Secretary of the Interior for purchase or rental under this Act, and to fix the price or prices at which such area may be purchased or rented; and no purchase or rental shall be made of any such area until it has been duly approved for purchase or rental by said Commission.

Any Member of the House of Representatives, who is a member of Congress, if reelected to the succeeding Congress, may serve on the Commission notwithstanding the expiration of a Congress. Any vacancy on the Commission shall be filled in the same manner as the original appointment. The ranking officer of the branch or department of a State to which is committed the administration of its game laws, or his authorized representative, shall be a member ex officio of said Commission for the purpose of considering and voting on all questions relating to the acquisition, under said sections, of areas in his State. For purposes of said sections, the purchase or rental of any area of land, water, or land and water includes the purchase or rental of any interest in any such area of land, water, or land and water.

Additional Act

In 1989, the Commission acquired the additional responsibility of approving project funding under the North American Wetlands Conservation Act. This Act provides Federal funding to encourage partnerships to protect, enhance, restore, and manage wetlands and other habitats for migratory birds and other fish and wildlife. The North American Wetlands Conservation Council, which was created by the legislation, submits project recommendations to the Commission for funding approval.

2011 Membership

Hon. Kenneth L. Salazar
Secretary of Interior, Chairman

Hon. Tom Vilsack
Secretary of Agriculture

Hon. Lisa P. Jackson
Administrator, Environmental Protection Agency

Hon. Thad Cochran
Senator from Mississippi

Hon. Mark Pryor
Senator from Arkansas

Hon. John D. Dingell
Representative from Michigan

Hon. Robert J. Wittman
Representative from Virginia

A Eric Alvarez
Secretary to the Commission
Telephone: 703/358 1716

The Migratory Bird Conservation Fund

The Migratory Bird Hunting and Conservation Stamp Act of March 18, 1934 (Duck Stamp Act) created the Migratory Bird Conservation Fund (MBCF) to provide the Department of the Interior with monies to acquire migratory bird habitat.

There are three major sources of funds deposited into the MBCF account. The most well-known source is the revenue received from the sale of Migratory Bird Hunting and Conservation Stamps, commonly known as Duck Stamps, as provided for under the Duck Stamp Act. The other two major sources include appropriations authorized by the Wetlands Loan Act of October 4, 1961, as amended, and import duties collected on arms and ammunition, as provided for under the Emergency Wetlands Resources Act of 1986.

The MBCF finances two Service land acquisition programs which are administered by the Division of Realty. The first program acquires waterfowl habitat in major migratory bird conservation areas under the authority of the Migratory Bird Conservation Act of 1929. The second program acquires small natural wetlands, grasslands, and interests, known as Waterfowl Production Areas, under the authority of the Duck Stamp Act. Waterfowl Production Areas are located primarily in the Prairie Pothole Region of the upper Midwest of the United States.

A total of $51,595,355 was available for obligation from the MBCF during fiscal year 2011. Disbursements for all MBCF land acquisition functions during the fiscal year totaled $51,347,486. This includes $24,564,497 for the acquisition of land and interests in land totaling 29,683 acres at major migratory bird conservation areas, and $24,039,399 for land and interests in land totaling 21,828 acres at Waterfowl Production Areas.

GADWALL

**Migratory Bird
Conservation Fund (MBCF)
Approvals for
Fiscal Year 2011**

Area Approvals: New Areas

Area	State	Approval Date	Acres
Dakota Grassland CA	South Dakota	09/14/11	448,975
Nestucca Bay NWR	Oregon	06/15/11	3,435
Total			**452,410**

Area Approvals: Boundary Additions

Area	State	Approval Date	Acres
San Bernard NWR	Texas	06/15/11	1,544
Total			**1,544**

Price Approvals

Area	State	Approval Date	Acres
Bear River MBR	Utah	09/14/11	1,841
Canaan Valley NWR	West Virginia	06/15/11	73
Dakota Grassland CA	South Dakota	09/14/11	2,794
Lower Hatchie HWR	Tennessee	03/09/11	625
Nestucca Bay NWR	Oregon	06/15/11	21
San Bernard NWR	Texas	06/15/11	1,544
Savannah NWR	Georgia	09/14/11	627
Tualatin River NWR	Oregon	03/09/11	32
Tualatin River NWR	Oregon	09/14/11	28
Tulare Basin WMA	California	03/09/11	656
Total			**8,241**

Price Re-Approvals

Area	State	Approval Date	Acres
Dahomey NWR	Mississippi	09/14/11	260
Total			**260**
Grand Total			*462,455*

Refuge Acquisition Program

Fee Title Acquisitions

Area	State	Acres	Cost
Bombay Hook NWR	Delaware	273	$455,000
Bear River MBR	Utah	272	$825,930
Cache River NWR	Arkansas	451	$1,435,500
Great Dismal Swamp NWR	Virginia	233	$1,409,000
Edwin B. Forsythe NWR	New Jersey	255	$500,500
Glacial Ridge NWR	Minnesota	8,238	$1,000,000
Humboldt Bay NWR	California	167	$1,238,240
Lower Hatchie NWR	Tennessee	838	$1,910,000
Umbagog NWR	Maine, New Hampshire	1,385	$1,334,000
Nestucca Bay NWR	Oregon	21	$105,000
Red River NWR	Louisiana	609	$806,925
Stone Lakes NWR	California	104	$400,000
San Bernard NWR	Texas	1,363	$894,017
Silvio O. Conte NF&WR	New Hampshire	672	$635,000
Tualatin River NWR	Oregon	32	$275,000
Trinity River NWR	Texas	161	$160,500
Upper Ouachita NWR	Louisiana	640	$1,280,000
Wallkill River NWR	New Jersey	41	$123,000
Total		**15,753**	**$14,787,612**

Permanent Easement Acquisitions

Area	State	Acres	Cost
Dakota Grassland CA	South Dakota	2,263	$1,297,075
Tulare Basin WMA	California	1,621	$3,185,000
Total		**3,884**	**$4,482,075**

Leases

Area	State	Acres	Cost
Dahomey NWR	Mississippi	260	$9,100
Halfbreed Lake NWR	Montana	640	$1,512
Lacassine NWR	Louisiana	653	$14,900
Lost Trail NWR	Montana	240	$262
Ouray NWR	Utah	3,845	$19,820
Panther Swamp NWR	Mississippi	640	$16,320
Red Rock Lakes NWR	Montana	3,266	$10,949
St. Catherine Creek NWR	Mississippi	502	$15,566
Total		**10,046**	**$88,429**
Refuge Acquisition Program Net Total		*29,683*	*$19,358,116*

Small Wetlands Acquisition Program

Waterfowl Production Areas

Permanent Easement Acquisitions

State	Acres	Cost
Minnesota	2,480	$2,669,007
Montana	1,927	$419,500
Nebraska	1	$0
North Dakota	4,472	$1,566,150
South Dakota	10,398	$5,806,098
Total	19,277	$10,460,755

Fee Title Acquisitions

State	Acres	Cost
Iowa	274	$1,274,300
Minnesota	6	$93,500
Nebraska	0	$0
North Dakota	7	$14,800
South Dakota	281	$400,000
Wisconsin	423	$2,191,500
Total	991	$3,974,100

Leases

State	Acres	Cost
Montana	1,560	$3,778
Total	1,560	$3,778
Small Wetlands Acquisition Program Net Total	*21,828*	*14,438,633*
Grand Total	**51,511**	**$33,796,749**

RINGNECK

BLUE - WINGED
TEAL

New Area
Boundary &
Boundary Addition
Approvals

Following are the National Wildlife Refuge System
approvals for Fiscal Year 2011.

New Area Boundary Approvals

Dakota Grassland Conservation Area
Aurora, Douglas, Edmunds, McPherson, and Walworth Counties, South Dakota

Nestucca Bay National Wildlife Refuge
Tillamook County, Oregon

Boundary Addition Approvals

San Bernard National Wildlife Refuge
Brazoria and Matagorda Counties, Texas

New Area Boundary Approval

Dakota Grassland Conservation Area

Aurora, Douglas, Edmunds, McPherson, and Walworth Counties, South Dakota

On September 14, 2011, the Migratory Bird Conservation Commission approved the 448,975-acre Dakota Grassland Conservation Area boundary, and granted price approval for the easement acquisition of 2,794 acres. The subsequent acquisition of one of the approved easements established the Refuge later that month.

Dakota Grassland CA is located in eastern South Dakota. It lies in the Central Flyway east of the Missouri River and will eventually extend into North Dakota. The refuge is part of the Prairie Pothole Region (PPR), a biome consisting of shallow wetlands surrounded by native prairie. Due to continued wetland and grassland conversion into cropland, the PPR is one of the most altered migratory bird habitats in the western hemisphere. One of the most important waterfowl producing areas, the PPR is often called the "Duck Factory," producing mallard, northern pintail, gadwall, northern shoveler, blue-winged teal, lesser scaup, canvasback, and redhead.

The Service will purchase both grassland conservation easements and wetland easements from willing sellers. All land under easement will remain in private ownership and may be hayed or grazed without restriction and farmed when dry from natural causes.

New Area Boundary Approval *Dakota Grassland Conservation Area*

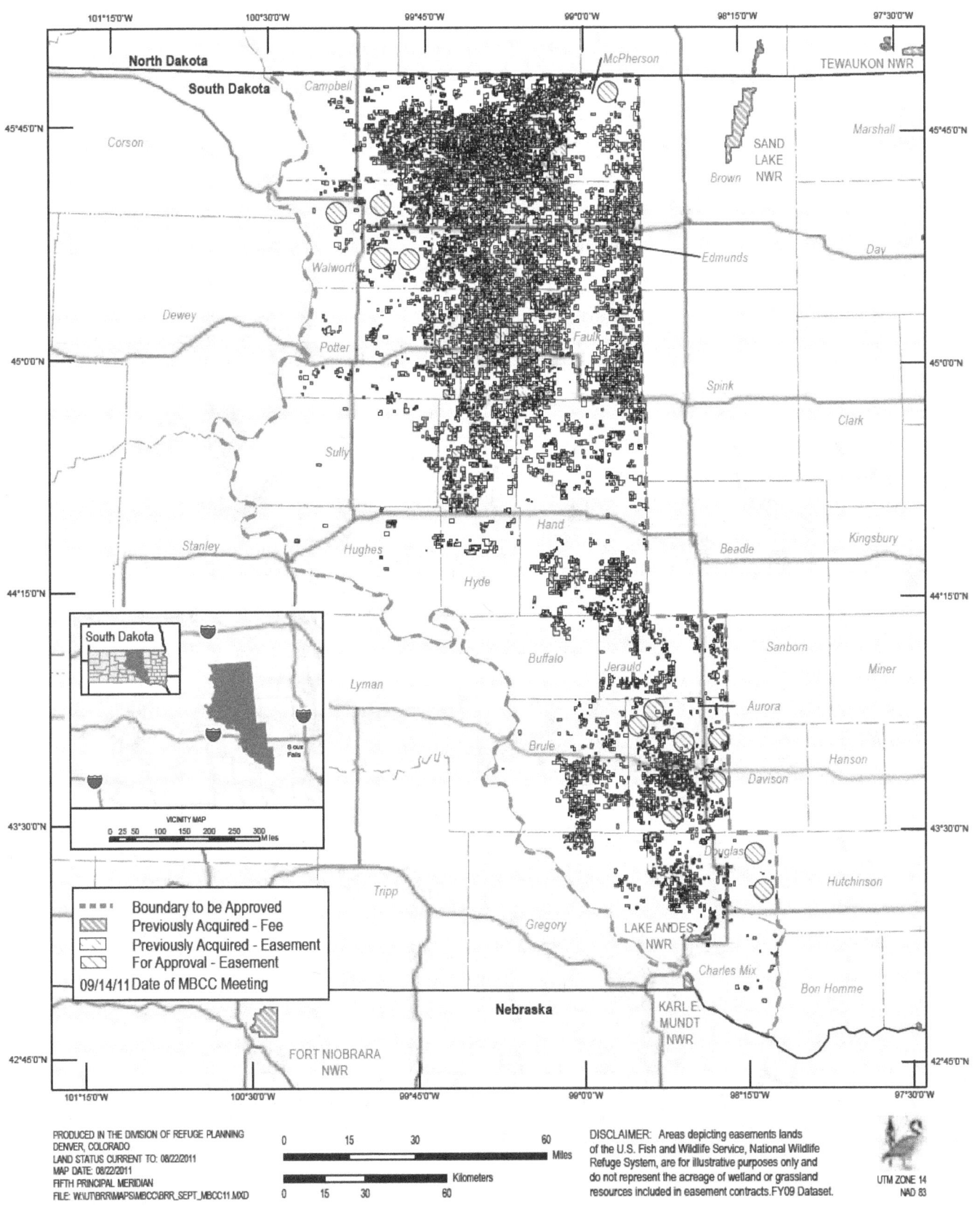

PRODUCED IN THE DIVISION OF REFUGE PLANNING
DENVER, COLORADO
LAND STATUS CURRENT TO: 08/22/2011
MAP DATE: 08/22/2011
FIFTH PRINCIPAL MERIDIAN
FILE: W:\UTBRR\MAPS\MBCC\BRR_SEPT_MBCC11.MXD

DISCLAIMER: Areas depicting easements lands of the U.S. Fish and Wildlife Service, National Wildlife Refuge System, are for illustrative purposes only and do not represent the acreage of wetland or grassland resources included in easement contracts.FY09 Dataset.

UTM ZONE 14
NAD 83

New Area Boundary Approval

Nestucca Bay National Wildlife Refuge

Tillamook County, Oregon

On June 15, 2011, the Migratory Bird Conservation Commission approved the 3,435-acre Nestucca Bay National Wildlife Refuge boundary, and granted price approval for the fee title acquisition of 21 acres.

Nestucca Bay NWR is located six miles south of Pacific City, Oregon. The Refuge was established to provide wintering habitat for dusky Canada geese and Aleutian cackling geese and to protect diverse coastal wetland habitats and upland habitat buffers for a variety of migratory waterfowl, shorebirds, raptors, songbirds, and anadromous fish. It supports 10-18 percent of the world's dusky Canada goose population and 100 percent of the unique Semidi Islands Aleutian cackling goose population, as well as mallard, northern pintail, American wigeon, and green-winged teal.

The acquired tract is on the south bank of the Little Nestucca River where it empties into Nestucca Bay. The tract was historically part of a large tidal saltmarsh system, but former owners diked, drained, and converted it to pastureland nearly a century ago. The Service will manage the diked lowland pastures to maximize forage production for wintering and migrating geese. The Service will restore native prairie and upland forests while allowing the tidal marsh, freshwater marsh, and bog areas to function naturally.

New Area Boundary Approval *Nestucca Bay National Wildlife Refuge*

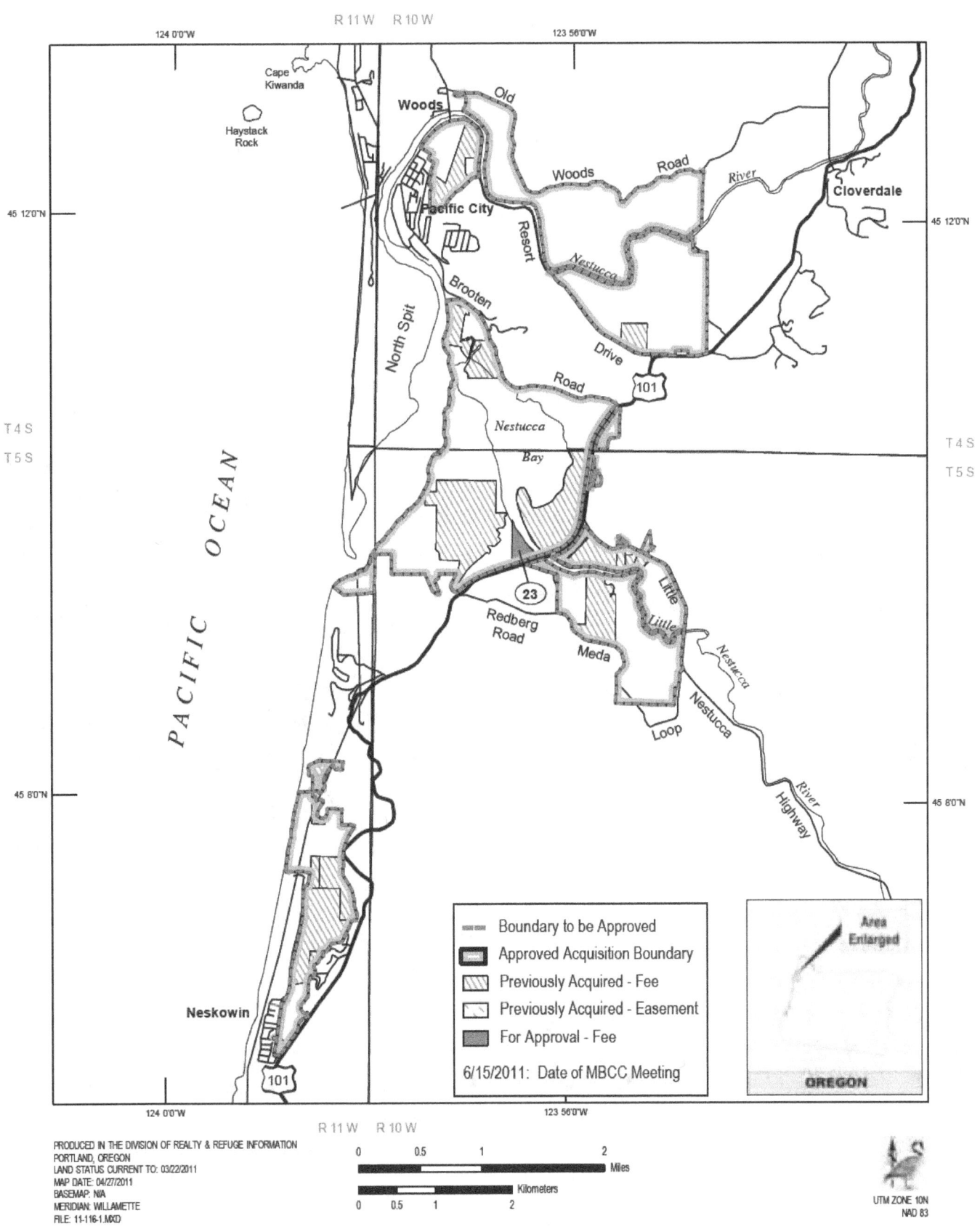

Legend

- Boundary to be Approved
- Approved Acquisition Boundary
- Previously Acquired - Fee
- Previously Acquired - Easement
- For Approval - Fee

6/15/2011: Date of MBCC Meeting

PRODUCED IN THE DIVISION OF REALTY & REFUGE INFORMATION
PORTLAND, OREGON
LAND STATUS CURRENT TO: 03/22/2011
MAP DATE: 04/27/2011
BASEMAP: NIA
MERIDIAN: WILLAMETTE
FILE: 11-116-1.MXD

UTM ZONE 10N
NAD 83

Boundary Addition Approval

San Bernard National Wildlife Refuge

Brazoria and Matagorda Counties, Texas

On June 16, 2011, the Migratory Bird Conservation Commission granted boundary and price approval for the fee title acquisition of two tracts, totaling 1,544 acres, at the Austin's Woods Unit of the San Bernard National Wildlife Refuge.

The Austin's Woods Unit is located 50 miles south of Houston, Texas. It is a productive and valuable wetland complex that provides habitat for migrating, wintering, and resident waterfowl, wading birds, neo-tropical migratory birds, and other wetland-dependent wildlife species. Thousands of waterfowl winter in the area, including mottled ducks, mallards, northern pintails, gadwalls, widgeons, northern shovelers, blue- and green-winged teal, black-bellied whistling ducks, and ruddy ducks.

The acquired tracts contain bottomland hardwood wetland forest and grasslands. The Service will manage the lands as habitat for waterfowl, wading birds, neo-tropical migrants, and other wildlife.

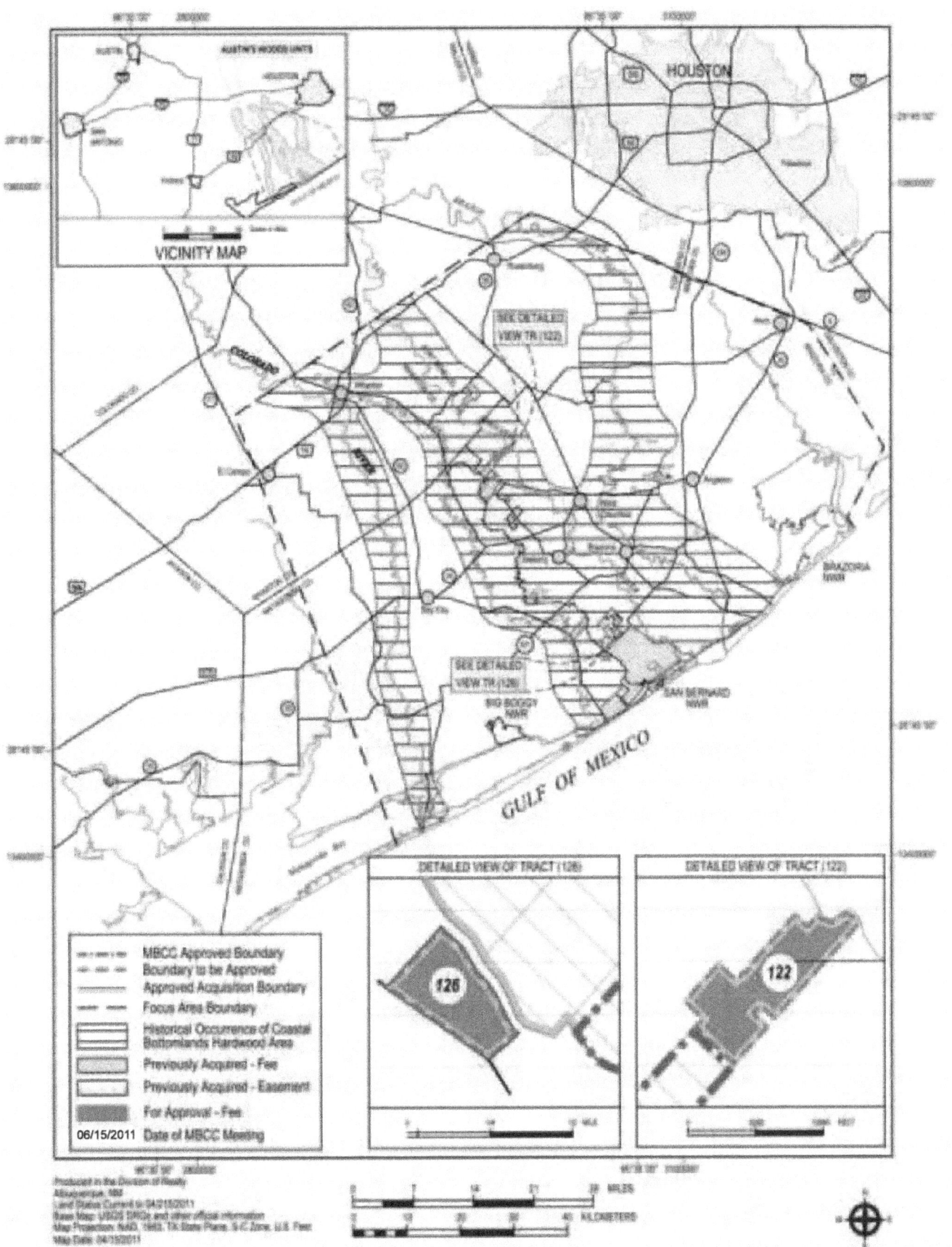

National Migratory Bird Refuges & Waterfowl Production Areas

The information contained in this report includes those acquisitions and dispositions of land and interests therein that are purchased with Migratory Bird Conservation Fund monies or acquired under the authority of the Migratory Bird Conservation Act. It also includes other migratory bird areas such as those that are transferred to the Fish and Wildlife Service under the authority of Public Law 80-537 to carry out a migratory bird management program.

Notes on Tables 1 and 2

In an ongoing effort to improve data quality, the figures in Tables 1 and 2 may show minor changes from previous annual reports. Lands in which the Service previously acquired a less-than-fee interest (leases and easements) may be purchased in fee during the year, and the number of easement or lease acres will show a decrease, and the number of purchased acres will show an increase. The acreage appearing in the Approvals section of this report will not appear in Tables 1 or 2 until after the Service acquires the tracts and expends the funds. Also, a newly approved refuge will not appear on Table 1 until the Service acquires the tract(s).

For information on all lands and interests under U.S. Fish and Wildlife Service control, refer to the Annual Report of Lands Under Control of the U.S. Fish and Wildlife Service. This report is available from the U.S. Fish and Wildlife Service, Division of Realty at <www.fws.gov/refuges/realty>, or by calling 703/358 1713.

WOOD DUCK

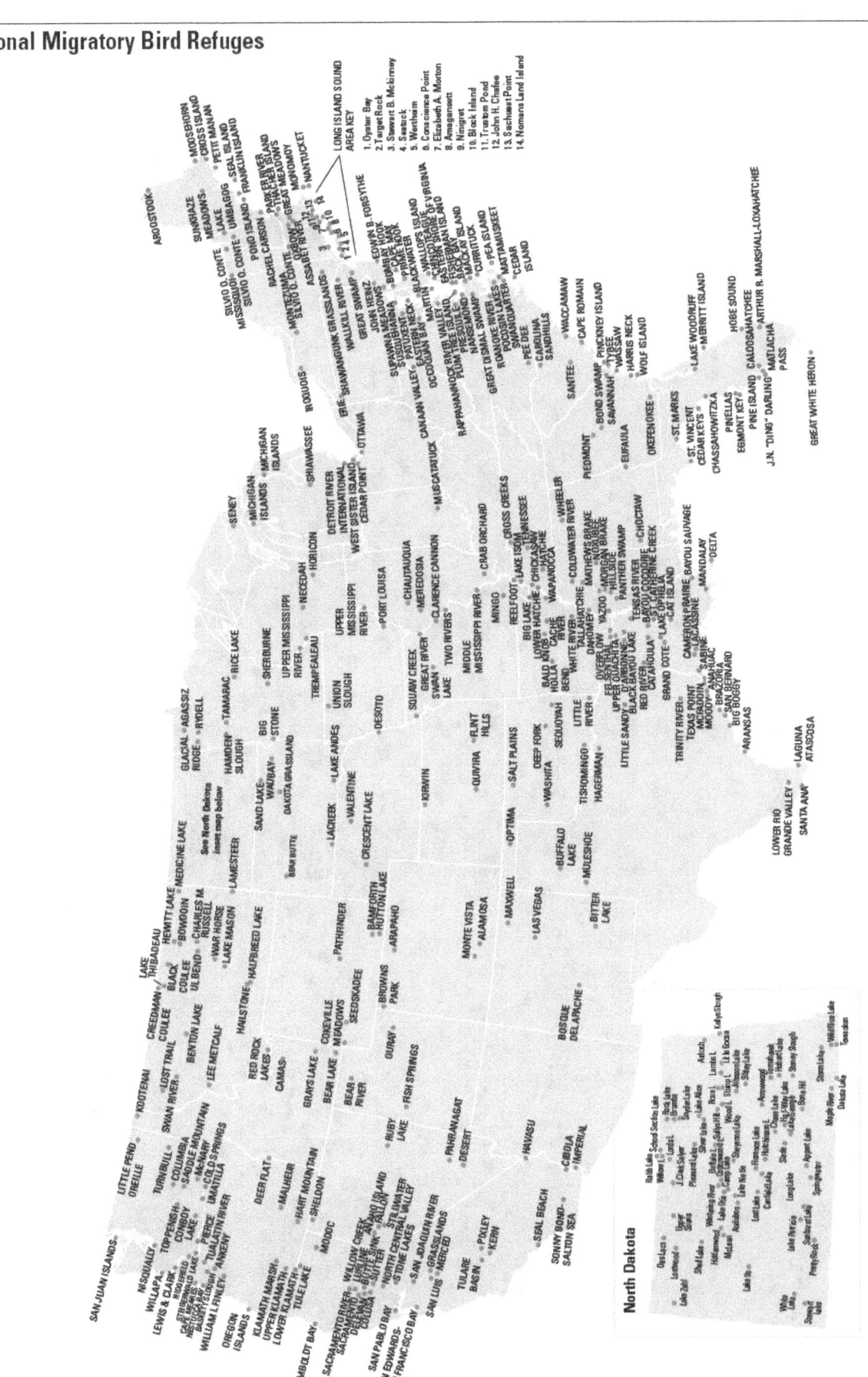

Table I. National Migratory Bird Refuges

State and Unit		FISCAL YEAR MBCF ACQUISITION				CUMULATIVE TOTALS AT END OF FISCAL YEAR					
		Purchased		Easement or Lease		MBCF				All Other Acres	Total Acres
						Purchased		Easement or Lease			
		Acres	Cost	Acres	Cost	Acres	Cost	Acres	Cost		
Alabama											
Choctaw		0.00	$0.00	0.00	$0.00	0.00	$0.00	0.00	$0.00	4,218.00	4,218.00
Eufaula	(1)	0.00	$0.00	0.00	$0.00	0.00	$0.00	0.00	$0.00	7,953.19	7,953.19
FSA Interest AL	***	0.00	$0.00	0.00	$0.00	0.00	$0.00	0.00	$0.00	742.69	742.69
Wheeler		0.00	$0.00	0.00	$0.00	0.00	$0.00	0.00	$0.00	34,430.66	34,430.66
State Total	3	0.00	$0.00	0.00	$0.00	0.00	$0.00	0.00	$0.00	47,344.54	47,344.54
Arizona											
Cibola	(2)	0.00	$0.00	0.00	$0.00	0.00	$0.00	0.00	$0.00	13,199.34	13,199.34
Havasu	(2)	0.00	$0.00	0.00	$0.00	0.00	$0.00	0.00	$0.00	30,279.82	30,279.82
Imperial	(2)	0.00	$0.00	0.00	$0.00	0.00	$0.00	0.00	$0.00	17,809.76	17,809.76
State Total	3	0.00	$0.00	0.00	$0.00	0.00	$0.00	0.00	$0.00	61,288.92	61,288.92
Arkansas											
Bald Knob		0.00	$0.00	0.00	$0.00	4,748.40	$3,427,000.00	0.00	$0.00	10,273.95	15,022.35
Big Lake		0.00	$0.00	0.00	$0.00	562.91	$31,854.69	0.25	$3.00	10,483.79	11,046.95
Cache River		451.23	$1,435,500.00	0.00	$0.00	49,463.77	$48,560,216.92	0.00	$0.00	19,030.18	68,493.95
Felsenthal		0.00	$0.00	0.00	$0.00	0.00	$0.00	0.00	$0.00	64,902.14	64,902.14
FSA Interest AR	***	0.00	$0.00	0.00	$0.00	0.00	$0.00	0.00	$0.00	3,458.67	3,458.67
Holla Bend		0.00	$0.00	0.00	$0.00	690.45	$336,903.00	0.00	$5,175.00	5,608.58	6,299.03
Overflow		0.00	$0.00	0.00	$0.00	13,416.75	$10,943,020.50	9.60	$0.00	0.00	13,426.35
Wapanocca		0.00	$0.00	0.00	$0.00	5,629.25	$1,528,416.00	0.00	$0.00	0.00	5,629.25
White River		0.00	$0.00	0.00	$0.00	10,371.88	$5,714,145.37	413.22	$22.00	148,372.50	159,157.60
State Total	8	451.23	$1,435,500.00	0.00	$0.00	84,883.41	$70,541,556.48	423.07	$5,200.00	262,129.81	347,436.29
California											
Butte Sink		0.00	$0.00	0.00	$0.00	514.98	$1,650,700.00	10,310.64	$12,816,903.00	217.88	11,043.50
Cibola	(3)*	0.00	$0.00	0.00	$0.00	0.00	$0.00	0.00	$0.00	5,245.33	5,245.33
Colusa		0.00	$0.00	0.00	$0.00	2,384.74	$107,313.30	0.00	$0.00	1,655.24	4,039.98
Delevan		0.00	$0.00	0.00	$0.00	5,796.54	$2,345,739.00	0.00	$175,000.00	0.00	5,796.54
Don Edwards San Fran. Bay		0.00	$0.00	0.00	$0.00	0.00	$0.00	0.00	$0.00	29,398.00	29,398.00
FSA Interest CA	***	0.00	$0.00	0.00	$0.00	0.00	$0.00	0.00	$0.00	6,673.24	6,673.24
Grasslands		0.00	$0.00	0.00	$0.00	6,442.28	$9,158,896.00	72,840.10	$40,224,459.00	12,556.27	91,838.65
Havasu	(3)*	0.00	$0.00	0.00	$0.00	0.00	$0.00	0.00	$0.00	7,235.34	7,235.34
Humboldt Bay		166.74	$1,238,240.00	0.00	$0.00	2,884.34	$6,492,650.00	0.00	$0.00	666.01	3,550.35
Imperial	(3)*	0.00	$0.00	0.00	$0.00	0.00	$0.00	0.00	$0.00	8,198.19	8,198.19
Kern		0.00	$0.00	0.00	$0.00	10,543.86	$579,912.00	0.00	$0.00	705.31	11,249.17
Lower Klamath	(4)	0.00	$0.00	0.00	$0.00	4,530.53	$3,390,123.00	0.00	$0.00	39,764.02	44,294.55
Merced		0.00	$0.00	0.00	$0.00	3,803.82	$2,180,000.00	0.00	$0.00	1.76	3,805.58
Modoc		0.00	$0.00	0.00	$0.00	5,359.58	$1,077,634.19	0.00	$0.00	1,711.65	7,071.23
North Central Valley		0.00	$0.00	0.00	$0.00	1,033.28	$4,445,531.00	9,446.32	$14,729,148.00	7,365.52	17,845.12
Pixley		0.00	$0.00	0.00	$0.00	0.00	$0.00	0.00	$0.00	7,156.66	7,156.66
Sacramento		0.00	$0.00	0.00	$0.00	10,775.61	$150,498.00	0.00	$0.00	43.39	10,819.00
Sacramento River		0.00	$0.00	0.00	$0.00	126.40	$145,000.00	0.00	$0.00	11,495.69	11,622.09
San Joaquin River		0.00	$0.00	0.00	$0.00	1,239.18	$7,030,819.00	0.00	$0.00	9,395.30	10,634.48
San Luis		0.00	$0.00	0.00	$0.00	7,422.41	$2,171,055.00	703.00	$2,284,000.00	10,337.00	18,462.41
San Pablo Bay		0.00	$0.00	0.00	$0.00	248.00	$243,400.00	0.00	$0.00	16,251.72	16,499.72
Seal Beach		0.00	$0.00	0.00	$0.00	0.00	$0.00	0.00	$0.00	910.71	910.71
Sonny Bono Salton Sea		0.00	$0.00	0.00	$0.00	9,342.14	$294,461.80	637.00	$1,089.27	27,679.73	37,658.87
Stone Lakes		104.43	$400,000.00	0.00	$0.00	214.61	$1,240,000.00	138.56	$365,800.00	6,058.90	6,412.07
Sutter		0.00	$0.00	0.00	$0.00	2,590.16	$291,281.80	0.00	$3,850.00	0.00	2,590.16
Tulare Basin		0.00	$0.00	1,621.00	$3,185,000.00	0.00	$0.00	2,663.00	$4,694,585.00	89.44	2,752.44
Tule Lake		0.00	$0.00	0.00	$0.00	0.00	$0.00	0.00	$0.00	39,116.58	39,116.58
Willow Creek-Lurline		0.00	$0.00	0.00	$0.00	0.00	$0.00	5,786.70	$7,173,433.00	14.10	5,800.80
State Total	24	271.17	$1,638,240.00	1,621.00	$3,185,000.00	75,252.46	$42,995,014.09	102,525.32	$82,468,267.27	249,942.98	427,720.76
Colorado											
Alamosa		0.00	$0.00	0.00	$0.00	10,904.78	$2,377,463.16	0.00	$24,035.90	1,121.59	12,026.37
Arapaho		0.00	$0.00	0.00	$0.00	17,811.33	$4,798,286.00	23.23	$35,358.66	7,686.84	25,521.40
Browns Park		0.00	$0.00	0.00	$0.00	5,275.63	$614,976.00	0.00	$68,118.76	6,874.25	12,149.88
FSA Interest CO	***	0.00	$0.00	0.00	$0.00	0.00	$0.00	0.00	$0.00	1,206.64	1,206.64
Monte Vista		0.00	$0.00	0.00	$0.00	13,950.66	$2,241,750.00	0.00	$0.00	883.33	14,833.99
State Total	4	0.00	$0.00	0.00	$0.00	47,942.40	$10,032,475.16	23.23	$127,513.32	17,772.65	65,738.28

Table 1. National Migratory Bird Refuges

State and Unit		FY MBCF Purchased Acres	FY MBCF Purchased Cost	FY MBCF Easement or Lease Acres	FY MBCF Easement or Lease Cost	Cum. MBCF Purchased Acres	Cum. MBCF Purchased Cost	Cum. MBCF Easement or Lease Acres	Cum. MBCF Easement or Lease Cost	All Other Acres	Total Acres
Connecticut											
Stewart B. Mckinney		0.00	$0.00	0.00	$0.00	361.24	$2,263,560.00	0.00	$0.00	585.94	947.18
State Total	1	0.00	$0.00	0.00	$0.00	361.24	$2,263,560.00	0.00	$0.00	585.94	947.18
Delaware											
Bombay Hook		273.00	$455,000.00	0.00	$0.00	15,551.48	$2,074,738.56	0.00	$1.00	779.28	16,330.76
FSA Interest DE	***	0.00	$0.00	0.00	$0.00	0.00	$0.00	0.00	$0.00	2.60	2.60
Prime Hook		0.00	$0.00	0.00	$0.00	8,286.06	$3,741,318.16	79.19	$5,346.20	1,775.95	10,141.20
State Total	2	273.00	$455,000.00	0.00	$0.00	23,837.54	$5,816,056.72	79.19	$5,347.20	2,557.83	26,474.56
Florida											
Arthur R. Marshall		0.00	$0.00	0.00	$0.00	2,549.77	$118,511.97	0.00	$0.00	141,404.00	143,953.77
Caloosahatchee		0.00	$0.00	0.00	$0.00	0.00	$0.00	0.00	$0.00	40.00	40.00
Cedar Keys		0.00	$0.00	0.00	$0.00	0.00	$0.00	0.00	$0.00	891.15	891.15
Chassahowitzka		0.00	$0.00	0.00	$0.00	22,556.82	$267,529.26	0.00	$0.00	8,286.09	30,842.91
Egmont Key		0.00	$0.00	0.00	$0.00	0.00	$0.00	0.00	$0.00	328.30	328.30
FSA Interest FL	***	0.00	$0.00	0.00	$0.00	0.00	$0.00	0.00	$0.00	3,057.15	3,057.15
Great White Heron		0.00	$0.00	0.00	$0.00	1,326.54	$906,195.00	0.00	$0.00	116,395.99	117,722.53
Hobe Sound		0.00	$0.00	0.00	$0.00	0.00	$0.00	0.00	$0.00	1,035.63	1,035.63
J. N. Ding Darling		0.00	$0.00	0.00	$0.00	541.98	$372,370.00	0.00	$0.00	5,864.81	6,406.79
Lake Woodruff		0.00	$0.00	0.00	$0.00	18,413.39	$1,340,310.75	0.00	$0.00	3,145.63	21,559.02
Matlacha Pass		0.00	$0.00	0.00	$0.00	0.00	$0.00	0.00	$0.00	564.73	564.73
Merritt Island		0.00	$0.00	0.00	$0.00	0.00	$0.00	0.00	$0.00	139,196.47	139,196.47
Okefenokee	(1)	0.00	$0.00	0.00	$0.00	0.00	$0.00	0.00	$0.00	3,724.48	3,724.48
Pine Island		0.00	$0.00	0.00	$0.00	0.00	$0.00	0.00	$0.00	602.24	602.24
Pinellas		0.00	$0.00	0.00	$0.00	0.00	$0.00	0.00	$0.00	394.35	394.35
St. Marks		0.00	$0.00	0.00	$0.00	30,985.17	$102,311.61	0.00	$0.00	38,253.40	69,238.57
St. Vincent		0.00	$0.00	0.00	$0.00	12,358.20	$2,035,000.00	0.00	$0.00	131.73	12,489.93
State Total	16	0.00	$0.00	0.00	$0.00	88,731.87	$5,142,228.59	0.00	$0.00	463,316.15	552,048.02
Georgia											
Bond Swamp		0.00	$0.00	0.00	$0.00	256.41	$1,000,000.00	0.00	$0.00	6,615.94	6,872.35
Eufaula	(5)*	0.00	$0.00	0.00	$0.00	0.00	$0.00	0.00	$0.00	3,231.00	3,231.00
FSA Interest GA	***	0.00	$0.00	0.00	$0.00	0.00	$0.00	0.00	$0.00	4,940.33	4,940.33
Harris Neck		0.00	$0.00	0.00	$0.00	0.00	$0.00	0.00	$0.00	2,822.68	2,822.68
Okefenokee	(6)*	0.00	$0.00	0.00	$0.00	344,341.83	$867,318.12	0.00	$0.00	55,052.99	399,394.82
Piedmont		0.00	$0.00	0.00	$0.00	473.97	$44,000.00	0.00	$0.00	34,493.01	34,966.98
Savannah	(7)	0.00	$0.00	0.00	$0.00	8,027.84	$1,705,352.40	0.00	$0.00	6,135.64	14,163.48
Wassaw		0.00	$0.00	0.00	$0.00	0.00	$0.00	0.00	$0.00	10,053.30	10,053.30
Wolf Island		0.00	$0.00	0.00	$0.00	4,587.82	$120,813.52	0.00	$0.00	538.00	5,125.82
State Total	6	0.00	$0.00	0.00	$0.00	357,687.87	$3,737,484.04	0.00	$0.00	123,882.89	481,570.76
Idaho											
Bear Lake		0.00	$0.00	0.00	$0.00	626.57	$212,279.30	0.00	$1.00	17,582.09	18,208.66
Camas		0.00	$0.00	0.00	$0.00	10,438.46	$202,700.84	0.00	$0.00	139.88	10,578.34
Deer Flat	(4)	0.00	$0.00	0.00	$0.00	242.89	$26,415.50	0.00	$0.00	10,584.68	10,827.57
FSA Interest ID	***	0.00	$0.00	0.00	$0.00	0.00	$0.00	0.00	$0.00	1,300.57	1,300.57
Grays Lake		0.00	$0.00	0.00	$0.00	4,038.18	$1,843,000.00	32.49	$4,518.30	16,054.41	20,125.08
Kootenai		0.00	$0.00	0.00	$0.00	2,774.15	$708,100.00	0.00	$0.00	0.14	2,774.29
State Total	5	0.00	$0.00	0.00	$0.00	18,120.25	$2,992,495.64	32.49	$4,519.30	45,661.77	63,814.51
Illinois											
Chautauqua		0.00	$0.00	0.00	$0.00	44.54	$2,525.38	0.00	$0.00	6,436.02	6,480.56
Crab Orchard		0.00	$0.00	0.00	$0.00	651.07	$0.00	0.00	$0.00	43,324.46	43,975.53
FSA Interest IL	***	0.00	$0.00	0.00	$0.00	0.00	$0.00	0.00	$0.00	335.40	335.40
Great River	(8)	0.00	$0.00	0.00	$0.00	1,559.87	$353,202.72	0.00	$0.00	5,550.76	7,110.63
Meredosia		0.00	$0.00	0.00	$0.00	0.00	$0.00	0.00	$0.00	3,400.80	3,400.80
Middle Mississippi River	(8)	0.00	$0.00	0.00	$0.00	0.00	$0.00	0.00	$0.00	6,370.98	6,370.98
Port Louisa	(19)	0.00	$0.00	0.00	$0.00	0.00	$0.00	0.00	$0.00	1,470.89	1,470.89
Two Rivers	(8)	0.00	$0.00	0.00	$0.00	796.17	$346,943.75	0.00	$0.00	7,237.03	8,033.20
State Total	7	0.00	$0.00	0.00	$0.00	3,051.65	$702,671.85	0.00	$0.00	74,126.34	77,177.99
Indiana											
FSA Interest IN	***	0.00	$0.00	0.00	$0.00	0.00	$0.00	0.00	$0.00	219.03	219.03
Muscatatuck		0.00	$0.00	0.00	$0.00	7,713.53	$3,582,837.72	0.00	$0.00	88.69	7,802.22
State Total	1	0.00	$0.00	0.00	$0.00	7,713.53	$3,582,837.72	0.00	$0.00	307.72	8,021.25

Table 1. National Migratory Bird Refuges

State and Unit		FISCAL YEAR MBCF ACQUISITION				CUMULATIVE TOTALS AT END OF FISCAL YEAR					
		Purchased		Easement or Lease		MBCF				All Other Acres	Total Acres
						Purchased		Easement or Lease			
		Acres	Cost	Acres	Cost	Acres	Cost	Acres	Cost		
Iowa											
Desoto	(10)	0.00	$0.00	0.00	$0.00	3,444.79	$639,117.53	0.00	$0.00	57.98	3,502.77
Port Louisa	(11)*	0.00	$0.00	0.00	$0.00	47.50	$16,000.00	0.00	$0.00	22,596.86	22,644.36
Union Slough		0.00	$0.00	0.00	$0.00	2,845.24	$210,406.69	70.70	$608.00	0.00	2,915.94
State Total	**2**	**0.00**	**$0.00**	**0.00**	**$0.00**	**6,337.53**	**$865,524.22**	**70.70**	**$608.00**	**22,654.84**	**29,063.07**
Kansas											
Flint Hills		0.00	$0.00	0.00	$0.00	0.00	$0.00	0.00	$0.00	18,463.36	18,463.36
FSA Interest KS	***	0.00	$0.00	0.00	$0.00	0.00	$0.00	0.00	$0.00	116.50	116.50
Kirwin		0.00	$0.00	0.00	$0.00	0.00	$0.00	0.00	$0.00	10,778.00	10,778.00
Quivira		0.00	$0.00	0.00	$0.00	21,820.10	$2,059,238.00	0.00	$0.00	199.20	22,019.30
State Total	**3**	**0.00**	**$0.00**	**0.00**	**$0.00**	**21,820.10**	**$2,059,238.00**	**0.00**	**$0.00**	**29,557.06**	**51,377.16**
Kentucky											
Reelfoot	(14)	0.00	$0.00	0.00	$0.00	2,039.64	$418,450.15	0.00	$0.00	0.00	2,039.64
State Total	**1**	**0.00**	**$0.00**	**0.00**	**$0.00**	**2,039.64**	**$418,450.15**	**0.00**	**$0.00**	**0.00**	**2,039.64**
Louisiana											
Bayou Cocodrie		0.00	$0.00	0.00	$0.00	5,222.20	$3,697,578.00	0.00	$0.00	9,496.31	14,718.51
Bayou Sauvage		0.00	$0.00	0.00	$0.00	2,027.40	$1,112,500.00	0.00	$0.00	22,670.46	24,697.86
Black Bayou Lake		0.00	$0.00	0.00	$0.00	88.60	$150,000.00	0.00	$0.00	4,433.71	4,522.31
Cameron Prairie		0.00	$0.00	0.00	$0.00	9,621.30	$5,090,650.00	0.00	$0.00	14,926.73	24,548.03
Cat Island		0.00	$0.00	0.00	$0.00	1,641.44	$2,576,000.00	0.00	$0.00	8,832.91	10,474.35
Catahoula		0.00	$0.00	0.00	$0.00	14,869.86	$2,190,082.25	0.00	$0.00	10,154.05	25,023.91
D'Arbonne		0.00	$0.00	0.00	$0.00	0.00	$0.00	0.00	$0.00	17,419.63	17,419.63
Delta		0.00	$0.00	0.00	$0.00	34,462.73	$233,324.17	0.00	$0.00	14,336.37	48,799.10
FSA Interest LA	***	0.00	$0.00	0.00	$0.00	0.00	$0.00	0.00	$0.00	10,873.54	10,873.54
Grand Cote		0.00	$0.00	0.00	$0.00	264.56	$876,173.00	0.00	$0.00	5,997.00	6,261.56
Lacassine		0.00	$0.00	0.00	$14,900.00	9,886.29	$999,156.43	640.00	$286,400.00	23,839.97	34,366.26
Lake Ophelia		0.00	$0.00	0.00	$0.00	3,064.90	$1,451,930.00	0.00	$0.00	14,496.56	17,561.46
Mandalay		0.00	$0.00	0.00	$0.00	0.00	$0.00	0.00	$0.00	4,619.73	4,619.73
Red River		609.00	$806,925.00	0.00	$0.00	3,541.43	$3,682,835.00	0.00	$0.00	9,474.50	13,015.93
Sabine		0.00	$0.00	0.00	$0.00	566.66	$14,000.51	0.00	$0.00	125,223.42	125,790.08
Tensas River		0.00	$0.00	0.00	$0.00	1,507.78	$1,220,227.00	0.00	$0.00	74,739.43	76,247.21
Upper Ouachita		639.60	$1,280,000.00	0.00	$0.00	42,823.18	$22,412,902.00	0.00	$1,823,540.00	3,921.91	46,745.09
State Total	**16**	**1,248.60**	**$2,086,925.00**	**0.00**	**$14,900.00**	**129,588.33**	**$45,707,358.36**	**640.00**	**$2,109,940.00**	**375,456.23**	**505,684.56**
Maine											
Aroostook		0.00	$0.00	0.00	$0.00	0.00	$0.00	0.00	$0.00	5,252.25	5,252.25
Cross Island		0.00	$0.00	0.00	$0.00	0.00	$0.00	0.00	$0.00	1,703.10	1,703.10
Franklin Island		0.00	$0.00	0.00	$0.00	0.00	$0.00	0.00	$0.00	11.94	11.94
FSA Interest ME	***	0.00	$0.00	0.00	$0.00	0.00	$0.00	0.00	$0.00	622.08	622.08
Moosehorn		0.00	$0.00	0.00	$0.00	19,782.52	$2,023,308.59	0.00	$0.00	9,552.21	29,334.73
Petit Manan		0.00	$0.00	0.00	$0.00	1,472.30	$350,000.00	0.00	$0.00	4,935.76	6,408.06
Pond Island		0.00	$0.00	0.00	$0.00	0.00	$0.00	0.00	$0.00	10.00	10.00
Rachel Carson		0.00	$0.00	0.00	$0.00	2,870.31	$1,539,347.75	2.97	$3,100.00	2,517.57	5,390.85
Seal Island		0.00	$0.00	0.00	$0.00	0.00	$0.00	0.00	$0.00	65.00	65.00
Sunkhaze Meadows		0.00	$0.00	0.00	$0.00	1,170.00	$250,500.00	0.00	$0.00	10,265.71	11,435.71
Umbagog	(36)*	275.27	$239,000.00	0.00	$0.00	3,993.24	$1,926,119.70	0.00	$0.00	3,934.16	7,927.40
State Total	**9**	**275.27**	**$239,000.00**	**0.00**	**$0.00**	**29,288.37**	**$6,089,276.04**	**2.97**	**$3,100.00**	**38,869.78**	**68,161.12**
Maryland											
Blackwater		0.00	$0.00	0.00	$0.00	20,491.19	$12,435,183.86	0.00	$0.00	6,755.72	27,246.91
Chincoteague	(16)*	0.00	$0.00	0.00	$0.00	417.81	$13,780.42	0.00	$0.00	0.00	417.81
Eastern Neck		0.00	$0.00	0.00	$0.00	2,286.27	$1,606,145.09	0.00	$0.00	0.00	2,286.27
FSA Interest MD	***	0.00	$0.00	0.00	$0.00	0.00	$0.00	0.00	$0.00	67.94	67.94
Martin	(16)	0.00	$0.00	0.00	$0.00	1,853.57	$61,027.00	0.00	$0.00	2,569.86	4,423.43
Patuxent		0.00	$0.00	0.00	$0.00	431.93	$7,667.57	0.00	$0.00	12,409.00	12,840.93
Susquehanna		0.00	$0.00	0.00	$0.00	0.00	$0.00	0.00	$0.00	3.79	3.79
State Total	**5**	**0.00**	**$0.00**	**0.00**	**$0.00**	**25,480.77**	**$14,123,803.94**	**0.00**	**$0.00**	**21,806.31**	**47,287.08**
Massachusetts											
Assabet River		0.00	$0.00	0.00	$0.00	103.38	$125,273.00	0.00	$0.00	2,229.20	2,332.58
Great Meadows		0.00	$0.00	0.00	$0.00	2,902.81	$2,209,918.90	0.00	$0.00	947.00	3,849.81
Monomoy		0.00	$0.00	0.00	$0.00	7,435.46	$18,339.00	0.00	$0.00	168.54	7,604.00
Nantucket		0.00	$0.00	0.00	$0.00	0.00	$0.00	0.00	$0.00	24.00	24.00
Nomans Land Island		0.00	$0.00	0.00	$0.00	0.00	$0.00	0.00	$0.00	628.00	628.00

Table 1. National Migratory Bird Refuges

State and Unit		FISCAL YEAR MBCF ACQUISITION				CUMULATIVE TOTALS AT END OF FISCAL YEAR					
		Purchased		Easement or Lease		MBCF				All Other Acres	Total Acres
						Purchased		Easement or Lease			
		Acres	Cost	Acres	Cost	Acres	Cost	Acres	Cost	Acres	Acres
Massachusetts (Continued)											
Oxbow		0.00	$0.00	0.00	$0.00	0.00	$0.00	0.00	$0.00	1,677.02	1,677.02
Parker River		0.00	$0.00	0.00	$0.00	4,617.79	$107,740.84	0.00	$0.00	109.42	4,727.21
Silvio O. Conte	(41)*	0.00	$0.00	0.00	$0.00	230.38	$371,361.00	0.00	$0.00	450.97	681.35
Thacher Island		0.00	$0.00	0.00	$0.00	0.00	$0.00	0.00	$0.00	22.00	22.00
State Total	**8**	**0.00**	**$0.00**	**0.00**	**$0.00**	**15,289.82**	**$2,832,632.74**	**0.00**	**$0.00**	**6,256.15**	**21,545.97**
Michigan											
Detroit River		0.00	$0.00	0.00	$0.00	283.95	$1,749,068.00	0.00	$0.00	5,476.51	5,760.46
FSA Interest MI	***	0.00	$0.00	0.00	$0.00	0.00	$0.00	0.00	$0.00	94.00	94.00
Michigan Islands		0.00	$0.00	0.00	$0.00	0.00	$0.00	0.00	$0.00	744.39	744.39
Seney		0.00	$0.00	0.00	$0.00	44,201.80	$127,726.66	0.00	$0.00	51,043.01	95,244.81
Shiawassee		0.00	$0.00	0.00	$0.00	8,376.46	$1,401,015.67	0.00	$0.00	1,178.05	9,554.51
State Total	**4**	**0.00**	**$0.00**	**0.00**	**$0.00**	**52,862.21**	**$3,277,810.33**	**0.00**	**$0.00**	**58,535.96**	**111,398.17**
Minnesota											
Agassiz		0.00	$0.00	0.00	$0.00	700.11	$40,226.04	0.00	$0.00	60,800.82	61,500.93
Big Stone		0.00	$0.00	0.00	$0.00	0.00	$0.00	0.00	$0.00	11,585.42	11,585.42
FSA Interest MN	***	0.00	$0.00	0.00	$0.00	0.00	$0.00	0.00	$0.00	2,561.80	2,561.80
Glacial Ridge		8,238.47	$1,000,000.00	0.00	$0.00	11,775.47	$2,000,000.00	0.00	$0.00	5,754.58	17,530.05
Hamden Slough		0.00	$0.00	0.00	$0.00	3,136.45	$1,832,872.00	73.40	$0.00	0.00	3,209.85
Rice Lake		0.00	$0.00	0.00	$0.00	6,435.60	$197,329.77	0.00	$0.00	10,036.68	16,472.28
Rydell		0.00	$0.00	0.00	$0.00	0.00	$0.00	0.00	$0.00	2,070.00	2,070.00
Sherburne		0.00	$0.00	0.00	$0.00	29,556.90	$3,273,341.05	0.00	$0.00	120.94	29,677.84
Tamarac		0.00	$0.00	0.00	$0.00	35,151.38	$612,159.93	0.00	$0.00	45.50	35,196.88
State Total	**8**	**8,238.47**	**$1,000,000.00**	**0.00**	**$0.00**	**86,755.91**	**$7,955,928.79**	**73.40**	**$0.00**	**92,975.74**	**179,805.05**
Mississippi											
Coldwater River		0.00	$0.00	0.00	$0.00	2,694.10	$2,198,450.00	0.00	$0.00	94.26	2,788.36
Dahomey		0.00	$0.00	0.00	$9,100.00	0.00	$0.00	260.00	$44,200.00	8,906.80	9,166.80
FSA Interest MS	***	0.00	$0.00	0.00	$0.00	0.00	$0.00	0.00	$0.00	18,268.64	18,268.64
Hillside		0.00	$0.00	0.00	$0.00	291.43	$164,500.00	0.00	$0.00	15,407.37	15,698.80
Mathews Brake		0.00	$0.00	0.00	$0.00	2,406.07	$1,691,446.00	0.00	$0.00	8.64	2,414.71
Morgan Brake		0.00	$0.00	0.00	$0.00	7,241.28	$4,517,482.20	0.00	$0.00	131.83	7,373.11
Noxubee		0.00	$0.00	0.00	$0.00	1,427.14	$145,413.05	0.00	$0.00	45,725.15	47,152.29
Panther Swamp		0.00	$0.00	0.00	$16,320.00	32,243.96	$20,453,483.00	640.00	$206,310.00	7,765.06	40,649.02
St. Catherine Creek		0.00	$0.00	0.00	$15,566.00	24,429.29	$12,925,167.00	502.10	$115,001.02	160.00	25,091.39
Tallahatchie		0.00	$0.00	0.00	$0.00	2,324.14	$1,361,000.00	0.00	$0.00	2,070.00	4,394.14
Yazoo		0.00	$0.00	0.00	$0.00	12,940.43	$2,659,743.78	0.00	$32,760.00	2.21	12,942.64
State Total	**10**	**0.00**	**$0.00**	**0.00**	**$40,986.00**	**85,997.84**	**$46,116,685.03**	**1,402.10**	**$398,271.02**	**98,539.96**	**185,939.90**
Missouri											
Clarence Cannon		0.00	$0.00	0.00	$0.00	3,736.04	$1,163,649.25	0.00	$0.00	14.44	3,750.48
FSA Interest MO	***	0.00	$0.00	0.00	$0.00	0.00	$0.00	0.00	$0.00	1,784.68	1,784.68
Great River	(11)*	0.00	$0.00	0.00	$0.00	1,119.78	$460,000.00	0.00	$0.00	988.15	2,107.93
Middle Mississippi River	(11)*	0.00	$0.00	0.00	$0.00	0.00	$0.00	0.00	$0.00	1,704.17	1,704.17
Mingo		0.00	$0.00	0.00	$0.00	21,535.95	$298,615.82	11.86	$27.00	113.24	21,661.05
Squaw Creek		0.00	$0.00	0.00	$0.00	801.32	$38,275.46	1.00	$0.00	6,612.57	7,414.89
Swan Lake		0.00	$0.00	0.00	$0.00	5,379.32	$355,193.19	0.00	$0.00	6,113.65	11,492.97
Two Rivers	(11)*	0.00	$0.00	0.00	$0.00	0.00	$0.00	0.00	$0.00	232.00	232.00
State Total	**4**	**0.00**	**$0.00**	**0.00**	**$0.00**	**32,572.41**	**$2,315,733.72**	**12.86**	**$27.00**	**17,562.90**	**50,148.17**
Montana											
Benton Lake		0.00	$0.00	0.00	$0.00	147.64	$5,315.00	60.94	$8,763.00	12,250.86	12,459.44
Black Coulee		0.00	$0.00	0.00	$0.00	0.00	$0.00	0.00	$0.00	1,308.88	1,308.88
Bowdoin		0.00	$0.00	0.00	$0.00	0.00	$0.00	0.00	$0.00	15,551.97	15,551.97
Charles M. Russell		0.00	$0.00	0.00	$0.00	0.00	$0.00	0.00	$0.00	916,106.79	916,106.79
Creedman Coulee		0.00	$0.00	0.00	$0.00	0.00	$0.00	0.00	$0.00	2,728.00	2,728.00
FSA Interest MT	***	0.00	$0.00	0.00	$0.00	0.00	$0.00	0.00	$0.00	2,065.12	2,065.12
Hailstone		0.00	$0.00	0.00	$0.00	0.00	$0.00	0.00	$0.00	920.00	920.00
Halfbreed Lake		0.00	$0.00	0.00	$1,512.00	3,279.02	$291,000.00	640.00	$31,938.20	399.22	4,318.24
Hewitt Lake		0.00	$0.00	0.00	$0.00	0.00	$0.00	0.00	$0.00	1,360.92	1,360.92
Lake Mason		0.00	$0.00	0.00	$0.00	4,100.45	$0.00	0.00	$0.00	12,714.07	16,814.52
Lake Thibadeau		0.00	$0.00	0.00	$0.00	0.00	$0.00	0.00	$0.00	3,868.48	3,868.48
Lamesteer		0.00	$0.00	0.00	$0.00	0.00	$0.00	0.00	$0.00	800.00	800.00
Lee Metcalf		0.00	$0.00	0.00	$0.00	2,696.29	$799,680.00	0.00	$0.00	103.23	2,799.52

Table 1. National Migratory Bird Refuges

| State and Unit | | FISCAL YEAR MBCF ACQUISITION | | | | CUMULATIVE TOTALS AT END OF FISCAL YEAR | | | | | |
| | | Purchased | | Easement or Lease | | MBCF Purchased | | Easement or Lease | | All Other Acres | Total Acres |
		Acres	Cost	Acres	Cost	Acres	Cost	Acres	Cost	Acres	Acres
Montana (Continued)											
Lost Trail		0.00	$0.00	0.00	$261.66	4,693.20	$1,728,205.00	1,029.04	$4,128.48	3,182.87	8,905.11
Medicine Lake		0.00	$0.00	0.00	$0.00	2,513.26	$25,460.00	0.00	$0.00	29,020.45	31,533.71
Red Rock Lakes		0.00	$0.00	0.00	$11,145.47	3,540.28	$4,167,191.00	3,266.32	$46,979.14	69,558.24	76,364.84
Swan River		0.00	$0.00	0.00	$0.00	1,568.81	$901,645.00	0.00	$0.00	0.00	1,568.81
UI Bend		0.00	$0.00	0.00	$0.00	9,688.19	$577,280.00	0.00	$0.00	46,401.37	56,089.56
War Horse		0.00	$0.00	0.00	$0.00	0.00	$0.00	0.00	$0.00	3,392.87	3,392.87
State Total	18	0.00	$0.00	0.00	$12,919.13	32,227.14	$8,495,776.00	4,996.30	$91,808.82	1,121,733.34	1,158,956.78
Nebraska											
Crescent Lake		0.00	$0.00	0.00	$0.00	3,710.00	$31,048.00	31.49	$3,189.00	42,253.86	45,995.35
Desoto	(19)*	0.00	$0.00	0.00	$0.00	3,660.32	$591,507.20	0.00	$0.00	663.88	4,324.20
FSA Interest NE	***	0.00	$0.00	0.00	$0.00	0.00	$0.00	0.00	$0.00	3,070.18	3,070.18
Valentine		0.00	$0.00	0.00	$0.00	6,158.34	$62,747.00	0.00	$0.00	66,939.75	73,098.09
State Total	2	0.00	$0.00	0.00	$0.00	13,528.66	$685,302.20	31.49	$3,189.00	112,927.67	126,487.82
Nevada											
Anaho Island		0.00	$0.00	0.00	$0.00	0.00	$0.00	0.00	$0.00	247.73	247.73
Desert		0.00	$0.00	0.00	$0.00	320.00	$5,600.00	0.00	$0.00	1,614,993.49	1,615,313.49
Fallon		0.00	$0.00	0.00	$0.00	0.00	$0.00	0.00	$0.00	17,901.94	17,901.94
Pahranagat		0.00	$0.00	0.00	$0.00	3,915.60	$500,000.00	0.75	$0.00	1,466.39	5,382.74
Ruby Lake		0.00	$0.00	0.00	$0.00	29,945.73	$208,437.25	0.00	$0.00	9,980.37	39,926.10
Sheldon	(4)	0.00	$0.00	0.00	$0.00	23,143.67	$2,002.00	0.00	$0.00	549,752.48	572,896.15
Stillwater		0.00	$0.00	0.00	$0.00	0.00	$0.00	0.00	$0.00	88,845.68	88,845.68
State Total	7	0.00	$0.00	0.00	$0.00	57,325.00	$716,039.25	0.75	$0.00	2,283,188.08	2,340,513.83
New Hampshire											
Silvio O. Conte	(42)*	672.00	$635,000.00	0.00	$0.00	2,610.00	$2,670,645.50	3.40	$2,054.50	4,767.63	7,381.03
Umbagog	(37)	1,109.64	$1,095,000.00	0.00	$0.00	8,531.39	$4,435,246.58	0.00	$1.00	11,354.53	19,885.92
State Total	1	1,781.64	$1,730,000.00	0.00	$0.00	11,141.39	$7,105,892.08	3.40	$2,055.50	16,122.16	27,266.95
New Jersey											
Cape May		0.00	$0.00	0.00	$0.00	4,564.56	$5,038,193.00	0.00	$0.00	7,496.66	12,061.22
Edwin B. Forsythe		254.70	$500,500.00	0.00	$0.00	40,002.73	$17,903,592.97	0.00	$1,300.00	7,311.94	47,314.67
Great Swamp		0.00	$0.00	0.00	$0.00	2,808.67	$3,577,691.05	0.00	$0.00	4,964.45	7,773.12
Supawna Meadows		0.00	$0.00	0.00	$0.00	2,526.83	$968,744.00	0.00	$0.00	746.52	3,273.35
Wallkill River	(39)*	41.05	$123,000.00	2.08	$1.00	1,382.51	$3,001,912.50	2.08	$1.00	4,012.37	5,396.96
State Total	4	295.75	$623,500.00	2.08	$1.00	51,285.30	$30,490,133.52	2.08	$1,301.00	24,531.94	75,819.32
New Mexico											
Bitter Lake		0.00	$0.00	0.00	$0.00	10,753.66	$52,304.00	0.00	$0.00	13,854.98	24,608.64
Bosque Del Apache		0.00	$0.00	0.00	$0.00	56,850.31	$125,311.00	0.00	$0.00	480.87	57,331.18
Las Vegas		0.00	$0.00	0.00	$0.00	8,672.08	$2,121,150.00	0.00	$0.00	0.00	8,672.08
Maxwell		0.00	$0.00	0.00	$0.00	2,791.69	$423,370.79	0.00	$0.00	906.90	3,698.59
State Total	4	0.00	$0.00	0.00	$0.00	79,067.74	$2,722,135.79	0.00	$0.00	15,242.75	94,310.49
New York											
Amagansett		0.00	$0.00	0.00	$0.00	0.00	$0.00	0.00	$0.00	35.84	35.84
Conscience Point		0.00	$0.00	0.00	$0.00	0.00	$0.00	0.00	$0.00	60.40	60.40
Elizabeth A. Morton		0.00	$0.00	0.00	$0.00	0.00	$0.00	0.00	$0.00	187.19	187.19
FSA Interest NY	***	0.00	$0.00	0.00	$0.00	0.00	$0.00	0.00	$0.00	2,714.10	2,714.10
Iroquois		0.00	$0.00	0.00	$0.00	10,757.81	$1,279,615.46	0.00	$0.00	70.25	10,828.06
Montezuma		0.00	$0.00	0.00	$0.00	7,937.78	$2,595,718.56	0.00	$0.00	1,221.32	9,159.10
Oyster Bay		0.00	$0.00	0.00	$0.00	0.00	$0.00	0.00	$0.00	3,204.08	3,204.08
Seatuck		0.00	$0.00	0.00	$0.00	0.00	$0.00	0.00	$0.00	209.23	209.23
Shawangunk Grasslands		0.00	$0.00	0.00	$0.00	0.00	$0.00	0.00	$0.00	566.53	566.53
Target Rock		0.00	$0.00	0.00	$0.00	0.00	$0.00	0.00	$0.00	80.09	80.09
Wallkill River	(40)	0.00	$0.00	0.00	$0.00	0.00	$0.00	0.00	$0.00	307.69	307.69
Wertheim		0.00	$0.00	0.00	$0.00	188.70	$193,217.80	0.00	$0.00	2,499.09	2,687.79
State Total	11	0.00	$0.00	0.00	$0.00	18,884.29	$4,068,551.82	0.00	$0.00	11,155.81	30,040.10
North Carolina											
Cedar Island		0.00	$0.00	0.00	$0.00	12,498.77	$389,171.21	0.00	$0.00	1,997.55	14,496.32
Currituck		0.00	$0.00	0.00	$0.00	3,762.23	$8,689,434.00	225.76	$120,000.00	4,331.70	8,319.69
FSA Interest NC	***	0.00	$0.00	0.00	$0.00	0.00	$0.00	0.00	$0.00	6,621.05	6,621.05
Great Dismal Swamp	(16)	0.00	$0.00	0.00	$0.00	2,790.60	$3,155,540.00	0.00	$1.00	24,811.80	27,602.40
Mackay Island	(16)	0.00	$0.00	0.00	$0.00	6,370.24	$1,172,606.95	0.00	$0.00	1,015.56	7,385.80

Table 1. National Migratory Bird Refuges

	FISCAL YEAR MBCF ACQUISITION				CUMULATIVE TOTALS AT END OF FISCAL YEAR					
	Purchased		Easement or Lease		MBCF				All Other Acres	Total Acres
					Purchased		Easement or Lease			
State and Unit	Acres	Cost	Acres	Cost	Acres	Cost	Acres	Cost		
North Carolina (Continued)										
Mattamuskeet	0.00	$0.00	0.00	$0.00	252.04	$1,285.35	0.00	$0.00	49,921.89	50,173.93
Pea Island	0.00	$0.00	0.00	$0.00	5,787.97	$40,401.86	0.00	$0.00	46.23	5,834.20
Pee Dee	0.00	$0.00	0.00	$0.00	8,438.94	$2,561,851.76	0.00	$0.00	27.66	8,466.60
Pocosin Lakes	0.00	$0.00	0.00	$0.00	12,350.35	$1,682,157.99	0.00	$0.00	97,756.29	110,106.64
Roanoke River	0.00	$0.00	0.00	$0.00	15,692.43	$8,338,258.00	0.00	$0.00	4,870.00	20,562.43
Swanquarter	0.00	$0.00	0.00	$0.00	15,492.76	$60,920.93	0.00	$0.00	918.33	16,411.09
State Total 10	**0.00**	**$0.00**	**0.00**	**$0.00**	**83,436.33**	**$26,091,628.05**	**225.76**	**$120,001.00**	**192,318.06**	**275,980.15**
North Dakota										
Appert Lake	0.00	$0.00	0.00	$0.00	0.00	$0.00	0.00	$0.00	907.75	907.75
Ardoch	0.00	$0.00	0.00	$0.00	288.13	$2,739.00	0.00	$0.00	2,408.00	2,696.13
Arrowwood	0.00	$0.00	0.00	$0.00	2,097.51	$46,906.58	0.00	$0.00	13,845.35	15,942.86
Audubon	0.00	$0.00	0.00	$0.00	0.00	$0.00	0.00	$0.00	14,739.19	14,739.19
Bone Hill	0.00	$0.00	0.00	$0.00	0.00	$0.00	0.00	$0.00	640.00	640.00
Brumba	0.00	$0.00	0.00	$0.00	0.00	$0.00	0.00	$0.00	1,977.48	1,977.48
Buffalo Lake	0.00	$0.00	0.00	$0.00	0.00	$0.00	0.00	$0.00	1,563.72	1,563.72
Camp Lake	0.00	$0.00	0.00	$0.00	0.00	$0.00	0.00	$0.00	584.70	584.70
Canfield Lake	0.00	$0.00	0.00	$0.00	3.10	$100.00	0.00	$0.00	310.13	313.23
Chase Lake	0.00	$0.00	0.00	$0.00	4,449.47	$25,611.00	0.00	$0.00	0.00	4,449.47
Cottonwood Lake	0.00	$0.00	0.00	$0.00	0.00	$0.00	0.00	$0.00	1,013.47	1,013.47
Dakota Lake	0.00	$0.00	0.00	$0.00	0.00	$0.00	0.00	$0.00	2,799.78	2,799.78
Des Lacs	0.00	$0.00	0.00	$0.00	631.63	$6,893.60	2.70	$0.00	18,912.81	19,547.14
Florence Lake	0.00	$0.00	0.00	$0.00	1,468.40	$31,485.00	0.00	$0.00	419.80	1,888.20
FSA Interest ND ***	0.00	$0.00	0.00	$0.00	0.00	$0.00	0.00	$0.00	6,936.40	6,936.40
Half-Way Lake	0.00	$0.00	0.00	$0.00	0.00	$0.00	160.00	$0.00	0.00	160.00
Hiddenwood	0.00	$0.00	0.00	$0.00	0.00	$0.00	568.35	$0.00	0.00	568.35
Hobart Lake	0.00	$0.00	0.00	$0.00	236.49	$5,165.00	0.00	$0.00	1,840.61	2,077.10
Hutchinson Lake	0.00	$0.00	0.00	$0.00	0.00	$0.00	0.00	$0.00	478.90	478.90
J. Clark Salyer	0.00	$0.00	0.00	$0.00	21,649.95	$306,352.60	50.52	$0.00	37,675.93	59,376.40
Johnson Lake	0.00	$0.00	0.00	$0.00	0.00	$0.00	0.00	$0.00	2,007.91	2,007.91
Kellys Slough	0.00	$0.00	0.00	$0.00	0.00	$0.00	0.00	$0.00	1,269.50	1,269.50
Lake Alice	0.00	$0.00	0.00	$0.00	8,027.86	$2,067,184.00	8.00	$0.00	4,059.68	12,095.54
Lake George	0.00	$0.00	0.00	$0.00	0.00	$0.00	0.00	$0.00	3,118.81	3,118.81
Lake Ilo	0.00	$0.00	0.00	$0.00	3,178.30	$78,582.98	0.00	$0.00	854.82	4,033.12
Lake Nettie	0.00	$0.00	0.00	$0.00	2,420.60	$148,245.00	0.00	$0.00	634.30	3,054.90
Lake Otis	0.00	$0.00	0.00	$0.00	0.00	$0.00	0.00	$0.00	320.00	320.00
Lake Patricia	0.00	$0.00	0.00	$0.00	0.00	$0.00	0.00	$0.00	800.23	800.23
Lake Zahl	0.00	$0.00	0.00	$0.00	3,178.98	$53,275.00	0.00	$0.00	644.21	3,823.19
Lambs Lake	0.00	$0.00	0.00	$0.00	0.00	$0.00	0.00	$0.00	1,206.67	1,206.67
Little Goose	0.00	$0.00	0.00	$0.00	0.00	$0.00	0.00	$0.00	288.41	288.41
Long Lake	0.00	$0.00	0.00	$0.00	12,578.82	$77,180.00	217.35	$10.00	9,702.33	22,498.50
Lords Lake	0.00	$0.00	0.00	$0.00	0.00	$0.00	0.00	$0.00	1,915.29	1,915.29
Lost Lake	0.00	$0.00	0.00	$0.00	0.00	$0.00	0.00	$0.00	960.21	960.21
Lostwood	0.00	$0.00	0.00	$0.00	3,148.01	$24,553.00	0.00	$0.00	24,440.57	27,588.58
Maple River	0.00	$0.00	0.00	$0.00	0.00	$0.00	0.00	$0.00	712.00	712.00
Mclean	0.00	$0.00	0.00	$0.00	344.00	$12,516.00	0.00	$0.00	416.00	760.00
Pleasant Lake	0.00	$0.00	0.00	$0.00	0.00	$0.00	0.00	$0.00	897.80	897.80
Pretty Rock	0.00	$0.00	0.00	$0.00	0.00	$0.00	0.00	$0.00	800.00	800.00
Rabb Lake	0.00	$0.00	0.00	$0.00	0.00	$0.00	0.00	$0.00	260.80	260.80
Rock Lake	0.00	$0.00	0.00	$0.00	0.00	$0.00	0.00	$0.00	5,665.96	5,665.96
Rose Lake	0.00	$0.00	0.00	$0.00	0.00	$0.00	0.00	$0.00	836.30	836.30
School Section Lake	0.00	$0.00	0.00	$0.00	0.00	$0.00	0.00	$0.00	297.30	297.30
Shell Lake	0.00	$0.00	0.00	$0.00	710.20	$17,902.00	0.00	$0.00	1,124.90	1,835.10
Sheyenne Lake	0.00	$0.00	0.00	$0.00	0.00	$0.00	0.00	$0.00	797.30	797.30
Sibley Lake	0.00	$0.00	0.00	$0.00	0.00	$0.00	0.00	$0.00	1,077.40	1,077.40
Silver Lake	0.00	$0.00	0.00	$0.00	0.00	$0.00	0.00	$0.00	3,347.64	3,347.64
Slade	0.00	$0.00	0.00	$0.00	0.00	$0.00	0.00	$0.00	3,000.20	3,000.20
Snyder Lake	0.00	$0.00	0.00	$0.00	0.00	$0.00	0.00	$0.00	1,550.18	1,550.18
Springwater	0.00	$0.00	0.00	$0.00	0.00	$0.00	0.00	$0.00	640.00	640.00
Stewart Lake	0.00	$0.00	0.00	$0.00	0.00	$0.00	0.00	$0.00	2,230.40	2,230.40
Stoney Slough	0.00	$0.00	0.00	$0.00	0.00	$0.00	0.00	$0.00	880.00	880.00

Table I. National Migratory Bird Refuges

State and Unit		FISCAL YEAR MBCF ACQUISITION				CUMULATIVE TOTALS AT END OF FISCAL YEAR					
		Purchased		Easement or Lease		MBCF				All Other Acres	Total Acres
						Purchased		Easement or Lease			
		Acres	Cost	Acres	Cost	Acres	Cost	Acres	Cost		
North Dakota (Continued)											
Storm Lake		0.00	$0.00	0.00	$0.00	0.00	$0.00	0.00	$0.00	685.90	685.90
Stump Lake		0.00	$0.00	0.00	$0.00	0.00	$0.00	0.00	$0.00	27.39	27.39
Sunburst Lake		0.00	$0.00	0.00	$0.00	0.00	$0.00	0.00	$0.00	327.51	327.51
Tewaukon		0.00	$0.00	0.00	$0.00	6,790.23	$460,122.00	0.00	$0.00	1,573.39	8,363.62
Tomahawk		0.00	$0.00	0.00	$0.00	0.00	$0.00	0.00	$0.00	440.00	440.00
Upper Souris		0.00	$0.00	0.00	$0.00	2,939.17	$41,220.00	3.76	$0.00	29,359.32	32,302.25
White Lake		0.00	$0.00	0.00	$0.00	1,040.00	$28,800.00	0.00	$0.00	0.00	1,040.00
Wild Rice Lake		0.00	$0.00	0.00	$0.00	0.00	$0.00	0.00	$0.00	778.80	778.80
Willow Lake		0.00	$0.00	0.00	$0.00	0.00	$0.00	0.00	$0.00	2,620.38	2,620.38
Wintering River		0.00	$0.00	0.00	$0.00	0.00	$0.00	0.00	$0.00	239.26	239.26
Wood Lake		0.00	$0.00	0.00	$0.00	0.00	$0.00	0.00	$0.00	280.00	280.00
State Total	62	**0.00**	**$0.00**	**0.00**	**$0.00**	**75,180.85**	**$3,434,832.76**	**1,010.68**	**$10.00**	**220,143.09**	**296,334.62**
Ohio											
Cedar Point		0.00	$0.00	0.00	$0.00	0.00	$0.00	0.00	$0.00	2,449.77	2,449.77
Ottawa		0.00	$0.00	0.00	$0.00	5,172.11	$2,572,893.55	590.80	$2.00	940.98	6,703.89
West Sister Island		0.00	$0.00	0.00	$0.00	0.00	$0.00	0.00	$0.00	80.13	80.13
State Total	3	**0.00**	**$0.00**	**0.00**	**$0.00**	**5,172.11**	**$2,572,893.55**	**590.80**	**$2.00**	**3,470.88**	**9,233.79**
Oklahoma											
Deep Fork		0.00	$0.00	0.00	$0.00	1,571.50	$421,000.00	0.00	$0.00	8,096.78	9,668.28
Little River		0.00	$0.00	0.00	$0.00	12,262.16	$9,881,540.94	0.00	$0.00	1,397.88	13,660.04
Optima		0.00	$0.00	0.00	$0.00	0.00	$0.00	0.00	$0.00	4,332.81	4,332.81
Salt Plains		0.00	$0.00	0.00	$0.00	1,117.39	$50,837.00	0.00	$0.00	31,079.92	32,197.31
Sequoyah		0.00	$0.00	0.00	$0.00	0.00	$0.00	0.00	$0.00	20,800.00	20,800.00
Tishomingo		0.00	$0.00	0.00	$0.00	0.00	$0.00	0.00	$0.00	16,464.18	16,464.18
Washita		0.00	$0.00	0.00	$0.00	0.00	$0.00	0.00	$1.00	8,075.37	8,075.37
State Total	7	**0.00**	**$0.00**	**0.00**	**$0.00**	**14,951.05**	**$10,353,377.94**	**0.00**	**$1.00**	**90,246.94**	**105,197.99**
Oregon											
Ankeny		0.00	$0.00	0.00	$0.00	2,796.33	$893,600.00	0.00	$0.00	0.00	2,796.33
Baskett Slough		0.00	$0.00	0.00	$0.00	2,492.33	$941,985.00	0.00	$0.00	0.00	2,492.33
Cape Meares		0.00	$0.00	0.00	$0.00	0.00	$0.00	0.00	$0.00	138.51	138.51
Cold Springs		0.00	$0.00	0.00	$0.00	386.88	$2,760.00	0.00	$0.00	2,729.95	3,116.83
Deer Flat	(21)*	0.00	$0.00	0.00	$0.00	0.00	$0.00	0.00	$0.00	187.94	187.94
FSA Interest OR	***	0.00	$0.00	0.00	$0.00	0.00	$0.00	0.00	$0.00	1,562.56	1,562.56
Hart Mountain		0.00	$0.00	0.00	$0.00	54,837.26	$216,114.58	0.00	$0.00	216,029.28	270,866.54
Klamath Marsh		0.00	$0.00	0.00	$0.00	18,288.86	$2,070,694.00	0.00	$0.00	22,756.32	41,045.18
Lewis And Clark		0.00	$0.00	0.00	$0.00	2,850.63	$469,250.00	0.00	$0.00	9,316.22	12,166.85
Lower Klamath	(2)*	0.00	$0.00	0.00	$0.00	0.00	$0.00	0.00	$0.00	6,618.13	6,618.13
Malheur		0.00	$0.00	0.00	$0.00	47,953.58	$2,461,939.35	0.00	$0.00	139,173.36	187,126.94
Nestucca Bay		20.81	$105,000.00	0.00	$0.00	20.81	$105,000.00	0.00	$0.00	979.06	999.87
Oregon Islands		0.00	$0.00	0.00	$0.00	0.00	$0.00	0.00	$0.00	748.55	748.55
Sheldon	(15)*	0.00	$0.00	0.00	$0.00	627.48	$4,079.00	0.00	$0.00	0.00	627.48
Tualatin River		32.00	$275,000.00	0.00	$0.00	453.31	$2,542,300.00	0.80	$4,375.00	1,732.03	2,186.14
Umatilla	(26)	0.00	$0.00	0.00	$0.00	0.00	$0.00	0.00	$0.00	8,907.37	8,907.37
Upper Klamath		0.00	$0.00	0.00	$0.00	4,146.10	$123,476.00	0.00	$0.00	20,836.58	24,982.68
William L. Finley		0.00	$0.00	0.00	$0.00	5,697.06	$2,600,006.00	8.94	$6,797.00	0.00	5,706.00
State Total	13	**52.81**	**$380,000.00**	**0.00**	**$0.00**	**140,550.63**	**$12,431,203.93**	**9.74**	**$11,172.00**	**431,715.86**	**572,276.23**
Pennsylvania											
Erie		0.00	$0.00	0.00	$0.00	7,962.81	$911,480.12	0.00	$0.00	837.42	8,800.23
John Heinz		0.00	$0.00	0.00	$0.00	80.33	$20,966.00	0.00	$0.00	912.84	993.17
State Total	2	**0.00**	**$0.00**	**0.00**	**$0.00**	**8,043.14**	**$932,446.12**	**0.00**	**$0.00**	**1,750.26**	**9,793.40**
Rhode Island											
Block Island		0.00	$0.00	0.00	$0.00	0.00	$0.00	0.00	$0.00	132.72	132.72
John H. Chafee		0.00	$0.00	0.00	$0.00	0.00	$0.00	0.00	$0.00	549.35	549.35
Ninigret		0.00	$0.00	0.00	$0.00	0.00	$0.00	0.00	$0.00	868.40	868.40
Sachuest Point		0.00	$0.00	0.00	$0.00	0.00	$0.00	0.00	$0.00	241.90	241.90
Trustom Pond		0.00	$0.00	0.00	$0.00	0.00	$0.00	0.00	$0.00	777.30	777.30
State Total	5	**0.00**	**$0.00**	**0.00**	**$0.00**	**0.00**	**$0.00**	**0.00**	**$0.00**	**2,569.67**	**2,569.67**
South Carolina											
Cape Romain		0.00	$0.00	0.00	$0.00	22,237.29	$17,218.18	0.00	$0.00	44,049.89	66,287.18
Carolina Sandhills		0.00	$0.00	0.00	$0.00	580.20	$38,352.75	0.00	$0.00	45,222.09	45,802.29

Table 1. National Migratory Bird Refuges

State and Unit		FISCAL YEAR MBCF ACQUISITION				CUMULATIVE TOTALS AT END OF FISCAL YEAR					
		Purchased		Easement or Lease		MBCF Purchased		Easement or Lease		All Other Acres	Total Acres
		Acres	Cost	Acres	Cost	Acres	Cost	Acres	Cost		
South Carolina (Continued)											
FSA Interest SC	***	0.00	$0.00	0.00	$0.00	0.00	$0.00	0.00	$0.00	1,430.04	1,430.04
Pinckney Island		0.00	$0.00	0.00	$0.00	0.00	$0.00	0.00	$0.00	4,052.70	4,052.70
Santee		0.00	$0.00	0.00	$0.00	4,322.43	$549,953.57	0.00	$0.00	8,193.98	12,516.41
Savannah	(1)*	0.00	$0.00	0.00	$0.00	7,991.40	$1,554,443.30	0.00	$0.00	7,019.97	15,011.37
Tybee		0.00	$0.00	0.00	$0.00	0.00	$0.00	0.00	$0.00	100.00	100.00
Waccamaw		0.00	$0.00	0.00	$0.00	1,292.41	$1,400,000.00	0.00	$0.00	21,627.47	22,919.88
State Total	6	**0.00**	**$0.00**	**0.00**	**$0.00**	**36,423.73**	**$3,559,967.80**	**0.00**	**$0.00**	**131,696.14**	**168,119.87**
South Dakota											
Bear Butte		0.00	$0.00	0.00	$0.00	0.00	$0.00	0.00	$0.00	374.20	374.20
Dakota Grassland	(49)	0.00	$0.00	2,262.71	$1,297,075.00	0.00	$0.00	2,262.71	$1,297,075.00	0.00	2,262.71
FSA Interest SD	***	0.00	$0.00	0.00	$0.00	0.00	$0.00	0.00	$0.00	151.00	151.00
Lacreek		0.00	$0.00	0.00	$0.00	9,379.75	$768,491.00	80.00	$35,933.00	7,395.58	16,855.33
Lake Andes		0.00	$0.00	0.00	$0.00	617.64	$92,322.00	0.00	$0.00	5,021.79	5,639.43
Sand Lake		0.00	$0.00	0.00	$0.00	3,917.39	$90,622.00	0.00	$0.00	17,902.80	21,820.19
Waubay		0.00	$0.00	0.00	$0.00	683.77	$23,838.00	90.53	$0.00	3,965.92	4,740.22
State Total	6	**0.00**	**$0.00**	**2,262.71**	**$1,297,075.00**	**14,598.55**	**$975,273.00**	**2,433.24**	**$1,333,008.00**	**34,811.29**	**51,843.08**
Tennessee											
Chickasaw		0.00	$0.00	0.00	$0.00	15,356.98	$17,796,888.72	0.00	$0.00	10,783.64	26,140.62
Cross Creeks		0.00	$0.00	0.00	$0.00	87.64	$26,200.00	0.00	$0.00	8,773.85	8,861.49
FSA Interest TN	***	0.00	$0.00	0.00	$0.00	0.00	$0.00	0.00	$0.00	685.39	685.39
Hatchie		0.00	$0.00	0.00	$0.00	11,220.73	$1,862,329.25	0.00	$0.00	335.37	11,556.10
Lake Isom		0.00	$0.00	0.00	$0.00	344.65	$27,290.72	0.00	$0.00	1,513.73	1,858.38
Lower Hatchie		837.86	$1,910,000.00	0.00	$0.00	8,313.66	$11,126,943.00	0.00	$0.00	4,793.90	13,107.56
Reelfoot	(22)*	0.00	$0.00	0.00	$0.00	496.53	$109,531.78	0.00	$0.00	7,914.17	8,410.70
Tennessee		0.00	$0.00	0.00	$0.00	430.45	$72,151.10	0.00	$0.00	50,929.01	51,359.46
State Total	6	**837.86**	**$1,910,000.00**	**0.00**	**$0.00**	**36,250.64**	**$31,021,334.57**	**0.00**	**$0.00**	**85,729.06**	**121,979.70**
Texas											
Anahuac		0.00	$0.00	0.00	$0.00	29,967.70	$12,452,064.20	63.09	$0.00	4,369.18	34,399.97
Aransas		0.00	$0.00	0.00	$0.00	49,235.68	$1,833,531.80	0.00	$0.00	65,421.37	114,657.05
Big Boggy		0.00	$0.00	0.00	$0.00	4,113.41	$2,374,594.19	258.23	$58,112.00	154.53	4,526.17
Brazoria		0.00	$0.00	0.00	$0.00	42,641.23	$13,822,482.26	0.00	$0.00	1,772.65	44,413.88
Buffalo Lake		0.00	$0.00	0.00	$0.00	0.00	$0.00	0.00	$0.00	7,664.16	7,664.16
FSA Interest TX	***	0.00	$0.00	0.00	$0.00	0.00	$0.00	0.00	$0.00	2,776.21	2,776.21
Hagerman		0.00	$0.00	0.00	$0.00	0.00	$0.00	0.00	$0.00	11,319.84	11,319.84
Laguna Atascosa		0.00	$0.00	0.00	$0.00	77,309.93	$12,475,079.19	0.00	$0.00	12,291.62	89,601.55
Little Sandy		0.00	$0.00	0.00	$0.00	0.00	$0.00	3,802.00	$0.00	0.00	3,802.00
Lower Rio Grande Valley		0.00	$0.00	0.00	$0.00	0.00	$0.00	0.00	$0.00	91,635.56	91,635.56
Mcfaddin		0.00	$0.00	0.00	$0.00	51,112.55	$10,956,489.20	7,748.88	$1,394,170.00	0.00	58,861.43
Moody		0.00	$0.00	0.00	$0.00	0.00	$0.00	3,516.87	$0.00	0.00	3,516.87
Muleshoe		0.00	$0.00	0.00	$0.00	2,154.80	$25,740.00	0.00	$0.00	4,294.30	6,449.10
San Bernard		1,362.59	$894,017.00	0.00	$0.00	37,832.80	$22,722,196.97	2.32	$1.00	9,596.03	47,431.15
Santa Ana		0.00	$0.00	0.00	$0.00	1,980.50	$23,766.00	0.00	$0.00	107.00	2,087.50
Texas Point		0.00	$0.00	0.00	$0.00	8,952.02	$1,719,000.00	0.00	$0.00	0.00	8,952.02
Trinity River		160.62	$160,500.00	0.00	$0.00	15,122.93	$12,327,402.99	0.00	$0.00	9,799.34	24,922.27
State Total	16	**1,523.21**	**$1,054,517.00**	**0.00**	**$0.00**	**320,423.55**	**$90,732,346.80**	**15,391.39**	**$1,452,283.00**	**221,201.79**	**557,016.73**
Utah											
Bear River		271.61	$825,930.00	0.00	$0.00	26,211.62	$4,405,049.47	45.76	$740.00	48,434.12	74,691.50
Fish Springs		0.00	$0.00	0.00	$0.00	3,774.82	$93,325.00	0.00	$73.00	14,217.42	17,992.24
FSA Interest UT	***	0.00	$0.00	0.00	$0.00	0.00	$0.00	0.00	$0.00	442.52	442.52
Ouray		0.00	$0.00	0.00	$19,820.00	5,014.98	$461,084.25	3,844.68	$475,183.15	3,116.90	11,976.56
State Total	3	**271.61**	**$825,930.00**	**0.00**	**$19,820.00**	**35,001.42**	**$4,959,458.72**	**3,890.44**	**$475,996.15**	**66,210.96**	**105,102.82**
Vermont											
FSA Interest VT	***	0.00	$0.00	0.00	$0.00	0.00	$0.00	0.00	$0.00	71.00	71.00
Missisquoi		0.00	$0.00	0.00	$0.00	6,324.65	$582,134.27	0.00	$0.00	905.04	7,229.69
Silvio O. Conte	(43)	0.00	$0.00	0.00	$0.00	17,189.21	$4,337,574.00	0.00	$0.00	9,515.80	26,705.01
State Total	2	**0.00**	**$0.00**	**0.00**	**$0.00**	**23,513.86**	**$4,919,708.27**	**0.00**	**$0.00**	**10,491.84**	**34,005.70**
Virginia											
Back Bay		0.00	$0.00	0.00	$0.00	7,482.09	$5,160,662.00	0.00	$0.00	1,675.58	9,157.67
Chincoteague	(23)	0.00	$0.00	0.00	$0.00	9,513.02	$635,403.91	0.00	$0.00	4,101.66	13,614.68
Eastern Shore Of Virginia		0.00	$0.00	0.00	$0.00	522.50	$1,844,370.00	0.00	$0.00	920.03	1,442.53

Table 1. National Migratory Bird Refuges

State and Unit		FISCAL YEAR MBCF ACQUISITION				CUMULATIVE TOTALS AT END OF FISCAL YEAR					
		Purchased		Easement or Lease		MBCF Purchased		MBCF Easement or Lease		All Other Acres	Total Acres
		Acres	Cost	Acres	Cost	Acres	Cost	Acres	Cost		
Virginia (Continued)											
Fisherman Island		0.00	$0.00	0.00	$0.00	825.00	$1,600,000.00	0.00	$0.00	1,071.30	1,896.30
FSA Interest VA	***	0.00	$0.00	0.00	$0.00	0.00	$0.00	0.00	$0.00	133.70	133.70
Great Dismal Swamp	(24)*	232.53	$1,409,000.00	0.00	$0.00	3,128.95	$4,233,762.98	0.00	$0.00	82,196.69	85,325.64
Mackay Island	(24)*	0.00	$0.00	0.00	$0.00	874.40	$26,855.75	0.00	$0.00	3.60	878.00
Martin	(23)*	0.00	$0.00	0.00	$0.00	0.00	$0.00	0.00	$0.00	145.62	145.62
Nansemond		0.00	$0.00	0.00	$0.00	0.00	$0.00	0.00	$0.00	422.99	422.99
Occoquan Bay		0.00	$0.00	0.00	$0.00	0.00	$0.00	0.00	$0.00	642.07	642.07
Plum Tree Island		0.00	$0.00	0.00	$0.00	0.00	$0.00	0.00	$0.00	3,501.68	3,501.68
Presquile		0.00	$0.00	0.00	$0.00	0.00	$0.00	0.00	$0.00	1,328.92	1,328.92
Rappahannock River Valley		0.00	$0.00	0.00	$0.00	1,287.30	$2,270,200.00	123.40	$585,001.00	7,307.72	8,718.42
Wallops Island		0.00	$0.00	0.00	$0.00	0.00	$0.00	0.00	$0.00	373.00	373.00
State Total	**10**	**232.53**	**$1,409,000.00**	**0.00**	**$0.00**	**23,633.26**	**$15,771,254.64**	**123.40**	**$585,001.00**	**103,824.56**	**127,581.22**
Washington											
Columbia		0.00	$0.00	0.00	$0.00	11,361.77	$426,346.04	0.00	$0.00	17,345.69	28,707.46
Conboy Lake		0.00	$0.00	0.00	$0.00	5,964.96	$2,289,100.00	718.29	$400,000.00	388.45	7,071.70
FSA Interest WA	***	0.00	$0.00	0.00	$0.00	0.00	$0.00	0.00	$0.00	1,471.75	1,471.75
Little Pend Oreille		0.00	$0.00	0.00	$0.00	4,216.65	$27,414.00	0.00	$0.00	38,376.92	42,593.57
Mcnary		0.00	$0.00	0.00	$0.00	185.16	$865.00	0.00	$0.00	15,372.93	15,558.09
Nisqually		0.00	$0.00	0.00	$0.00	2,494.24	$3,861,990.17	0.55	$3,000.00	1,905.20	4,399.99
Pierce		0.00	$0.00	0.00	$0.00	0.00	$0.00	0.00	$0.00	329.38	329.38
Ridgefield		0.00	$0.00	0.00	$0.00	4,670.16	$4,033,600.00	1.74	$21.00	556.20	5,228.10
Saddle Mountain		0.00	$0.00	0.00	$0.00	0.00	$0.00	0.00	$0.00	161,485.93	161,485.93
San Juan Islands		0.00	$0.00	0.00	$0.00	0.00	$0.00	0.00	$0.00	448.50	448.50
Steigerwald Lake		0.00	$0.00	0.00	$0.00	50.00	$500,000.00	0.00	$0.00	996.02	1,046.02
Toppenish		0.00	$0.00	0.00	$0.00	1,762.80	$599,137.00	1.29	$0.00	214.75	1,978.84
Turnbull		0.00	$0.00	0.00	$0.00	13,909.32	$507,411.38	0.00	$0.00	4,707.18	18,616.50
Umatilla	(4)*	0.00	$0.00	0.00	$0.00	0.00	$0.00	0.00	$0.00	14,875.83	14,875.83
Willapa		0.00	$0.00	0.00	$0.00	8,616.42	$5,122,010.74	0.12	$0.00	7,819.09	16,435.63
State Total	**13**	**0.00**	**$0.00**	**0.00**	**$0.00**	**53,231.48**	**$17,367,874.33**	**721.99**	**$403,021.00**	**266,293.82**	**320,247.29**
West Virginia											
Canaan Valley		0.00	$0.00	0.00	$0.00	635.14	$1,804,884.98	0.00	$0.00	15,855.45	16,490.59
FSA Interest WV	***	0.00	$0.00	0.00	$0.00	0.00	$0.00	0.00	$0.00	8.37	8.37
State Total	**1**	**0.00**	**$0.00**	**0.00**	**$0.00**	**635.14**	**$1,804,884.98**	**0.00**	**$0.00**	**15,863.82**	**16,498.96**
Wisconsin											
FSA Interest WI	***	0.00	$0.00	0.00	$0.00	0.00	$0.00	0.00	$0.00	920.00	920.00
Horicon		0.00	$0.00	0.00	$0.00	21,098.37	$555,238.34	29.00	$356.00	286.59	21,413.96
Necedah		0.00	$0.00	0.00	$0.00	244.92	$3,194.26	0.00	$0.00	43,470.94	43,715.86
Trempealeau		0.00	$0.00	0.00	$0.00	593.89	$0.00	0.00	$0.00	5,605.44	6,199.33
State Total	**3**	**0.00**	**$0.00**	**0.00**	**$0.00**	**21,937.18**	**$558,432.60**	**29.00**	**$356.00**	**50,282.97**	**72,249.15**
Wyoming											
Bamforth		0.00	$0.00	0.00	$0.00	964.80	$6,368.00	0.00	$0.00	201.23	1,166.03
Cokeville Meadows		0.00	$0.00	0.00	$0.00	4,738.89	$2,101,412.61	320.00	$36,037.42	4,200.43	9,259.32
FSA Interest WY	***	0.00	$0.00	0.00	$0.00	0.00	$0.00	0.00	$0.00	3,287.75	3,287.75
Hutton Lake		0.00	$0.00	0.00	$0.00	1,815.49	$7,944.00	0.00	$0.00	152.85	1,968.34
Pathfinder		0.00	$0.00	0.00	$0.00	0.00	$0.00	0.00	$0.00	16,806.90	16,806.90
Seedskadee		0.00	$0.00	0.00	$0.00	0.00	$0.00	0.00	$0.00	27,232.72	27,232.72
State Total	**5**	**0.00**	**$0.00**	**0.00**	**$0.00**	**7,519.18**	**$2,115,724.61**	**320.00**	**$36,037.42**	**51,881.88**	**59,721.06**
Grand Total	**370**	**15,753.15**	**$14,787,612.00**	**3,885.79**	**$4,570,701.13**	**2,359,576.77**	**$563,455,294.94**	**135,065.79**	**$89,638,036.00**	**7,676,537.11**	**10,171,179.67**

(1)	Also in	Georgia	(16)	Also in	Virginia	
(2)	" "	California	(17)	" "	New Mexico	
(3)	" "	Arizona	(18)	" "	Illinois, Iowa and Wisconsin	
(4)	" "	Oregon	(19)	" "	Iowa	
(5)	" "	Alabama	(20)	" "	South Dakota	
(6)	" "	Florida	(21)	" "	Idaho	
(7)	" "	South Carolina	(22)	" "	Kentucky	
(8)	" "	Missouri	(23)	" "	Maryland	
(9)	" "	Iowa, Minnesota and Wisconsin	(24)	" "	North Carolina	
(10)	" "	Nebraska	(25)	" "	Illinois, Iowa and Minnesota	
(11)	" "	Illinois	(26)	" "	Washington	
(12)	" "	Texas	(27)	" "	Mississippi	
(13)	" "	Illinois, Minnesota and Wisconsin	(28)	" "	Louisiana	
(14)	" "	Tennessee	(34)	" "	West Virginia and Kentucky	
(15)	" "	Nevada	(35)	" "	Pennsylvania and Kentucky	

(36)	Also in	New Hampshire
(37)	" "	Maine
(38)	" "	West Virginia and Pennsylvania
(39)	" "	New York
(40)	" "	New Jersey
(41)	" "	New Hampshire and Vermont
(42)	" "	Massachusetts and Vermont
(43)	" "	Massachusetts and New Hampshire

* - Counted in another state
** - Denotes interests transferred by the FSA
FSA - Farm Service Agency (Formerly Farmers Home Administration, Department of Agriculture)*

Wetland Management Districts Map

Wetland Management Districts are comprised of counties in which the Service has acquired or is leasing any wetland or pothole area and is managing them as a Waterfowl Production Area (WPA).

The different colors denote the different Districts.

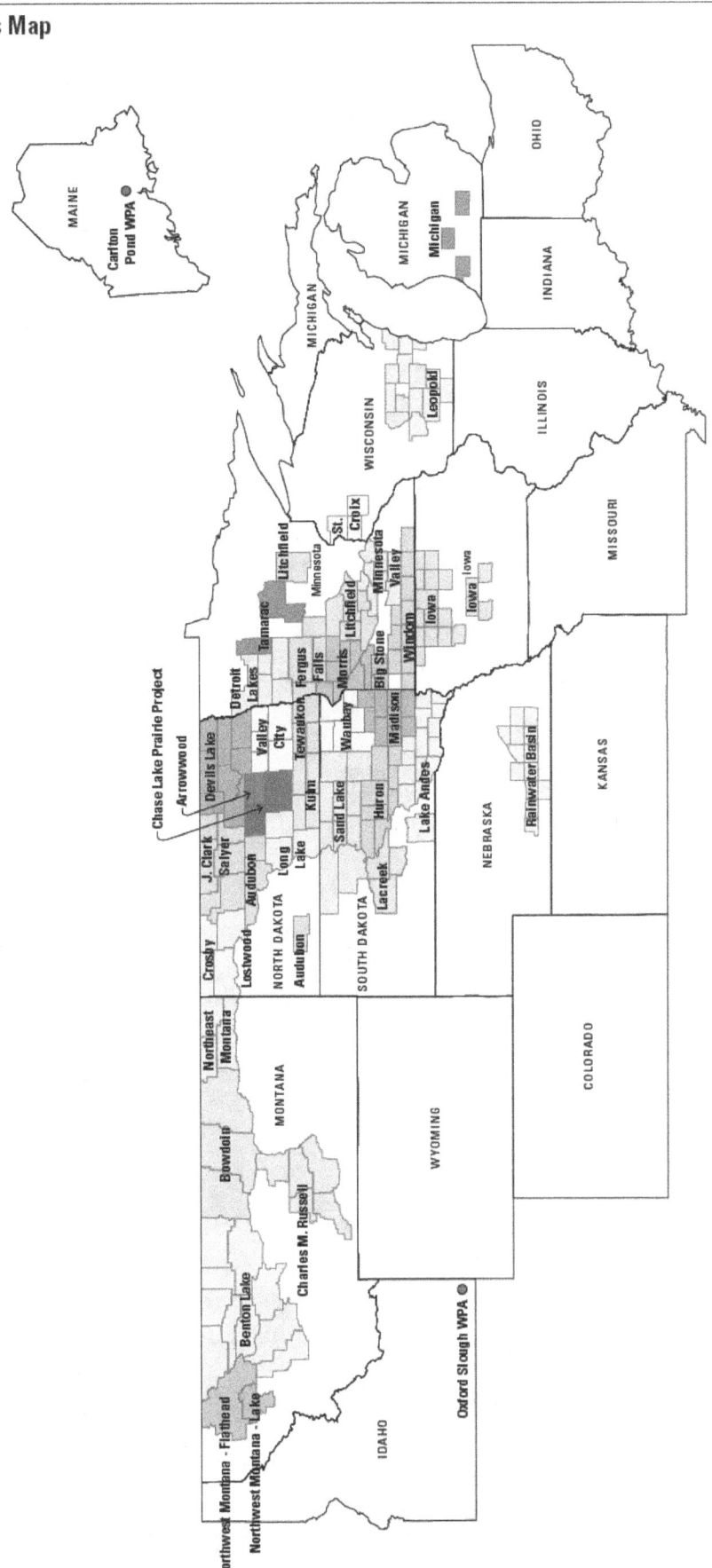

Table 2. Waterfowl Production Areas

State and Unit		FISCAL YEAR MBCF ACQUISITION				CUMULATIVE TOTALS AT END OF FISCAL YEAR					
		Purchased		Easement or Lease		MBCF Purchased		Easement or Lease		All Other Acres	Total Acres
		Acres	Cost	Acres	Cost	Acres	Cost	Acres	Cost		
Idaho											
Oxford Slough WPA		0.00	$0.00	0.00	$0.00	1,878.41	$530,000.00	0.00	$0.00	0.00	1,878.41
State Total	1	0.00	$0.00	0.00	$0.00	1,878.41	$530,000.00	0.00	$0.00	0.00	1,878.41
Iowa											
Iowa WMD											
Boone		0.00	$0.00	0.00	$0.00	391.33	$599,600.00	0.00	$0.00	0.00	391.33
Buena Vista		0.00	$0.00	0.00	$0.00	69.09	$169,000.00	0.00	$0.00	0.00	69.09
Cerro Gordo		0.00	$0.00	0.00	$0.00	2,720.25	$3,284,677.82	5.70	$10,200.00	0.00	2,725.95
Clay		0.00	$0.00	0.00	$0.00	920.53	$1,346,106.85	0.00	$0.00	0.00	920.53
Dickinson		216.75	$1,054,800.00	0.00	$0.00	5,518.61	$9,408,256.00	84.00	$37,725.00	635.34	6,237.95
Emmet		0.00	$0.00	0.00	$0.00	1,855.29	$2,417,575.00	16.00	$40,000.00	249.99	2,121.28
Greene		0.00	$0.00	0.00	$0.00	1,133.43	$3,305,500.00	0.00	$0.00	0.00	1,133.43
Guthrie		0.00	$0.00	0.00	$0.00	302.53	$609,740.00	0.00	$0.00	0.00	302.53
Hancock		0.00	$0.00	0.00	$0.00	802.70	$545,480.26	7.00	$2,250.00	0.00	809.70
Kossuth		0.00	$0.00	0.00	$0.00	3,519.86	$7,995,046.98	23.00	$28,775.00	0.00	3,542.86
Osceola		0.00	$0.00	0.00	$0.00	0.00	$0.00	37.00	$17,250.00	4.00	41.00
Palo Alto		57.45	$219,500.00	0.00	$0.00	731.81	$1,180,592.65	176.00	$222,850.00	58.00	965.81
Pocahontas		0.00	$0.00	0.00	$0.00	654.16	$1,716,400.00	0.00	$0.00	0.00	654.16
Polk		0.00	$0.00	0.00	$0.00	110.00	$241,500.00	0.00	$0.00	0.00	110.00
Sac		0.00	$0.00	0.00	$0.00	930.45	$2,493,280.00	0.00	$0.00	3.97	934.42
Winnebago		0.00	$0.00	0.00	$0.00	1,016.95	$1,138,300.31	105.00	$54,025.00	0.00	1,121.95
Worth		0.00	$0.00	0.00	$0.00	1,491.84	$1,088,329.87	18.00	$9,250.00	0.00	1,509.84
Wright		0.00	$0.00	0.00	$0.00	1,696.65	$2,615,725.00	0.00	$0.00	0.00	1,696.65
WMD Total:	*18*	*274.20*	*$1,274,300.00*	*0.00*	*$0.00*	*23,865.48*	*$40,155,110.74*	*471.70*	*$422,325.00*	*951.30*	*25,288.48*
State Total	18	274.20	$1,274,300.00	0.00	$0.00	23,865.48	$40,155,110.74	471.70	$422,325.00	951.30	25,288.48
Maine											
Carlton Pond WPA		0.00	$0.00	0.00	$0.00	1,068.21	$18,277.08	0.00	$0.00	0.00	1,068.21
State Total	1	0.00	$0.00	0.00	$0.00	1,068.21	$18,277.08	0.00	$0.00	0.00	1,068.21
Michigan											
Michigan WMD											
Barry		0.00	$0.00	0.00	$0.00	110.00	$550,000.00	0.00	$0.00	50.00	160.00
Jackson		0.00	$0.00	0.00	$0.00	160.00	$170,000.00	0.00	$0.00	138.41	298.41
Van Buren		0.00	$0.00	0.00	$0.00	77.08	$43,600.00	0.00	$0.00	0.00	77.08
WMD Total:	*3*	*0.00*	*$0.00*	*0.00*	*$0.00*	*347.08*	*$763,600.00*	*0.00*	*$0.00*	*188.41*	*535.49*
State Total	3	0.00	$0.00	0.00	$0.00	347.08	$763,600.00	0.00	$0.00	188.41	535.49
Minnesota											
Big Stone WMD											
Lincoln		0.00	$0.00	118.12	$152,300.00	1,094.01	$846,200.00	1,781.13	$1,272,346.04	0.00	2,875.14
Lyon		0.00	$0.00	30.00	$61,075.00	1,791.22	$2,042,220.00	391.20	$238,105.00	0.00	2,182.42
WMD Total:	*2*	*0.00*	*$0.00*	*148.12*	*$213,375.00*	*2,885.23*	*$2,888,420.00*	*2,172.33*	*$1,510,451.04*	*0.00*	*5,057.56*
Detroit Lakes WMD											
Becker		0.00	$0.00	0.00	$0.00	13,213.33	$5,379,470.56	2,866.93	$1,375,560.00	6.33	16,086.59
Clay		0.00	$0.00	17.16	$18,800.00	10,726.36	$3,520,045.18	3,596.30	$907,272.15	21.35	14,344.01
Mahnomen		0.00	$0.00	364.13	$239,475.00	6,087.33	$1,183,558.90	5,168.54	$419,361.00	957.00	12,212.87
Norman		0.00	$0.00	0.00	$0.00	1,120.00	$400,000.00	0.00	$0.00	0.00	1,120.00
Polk		0.00	$0.00	141.71	$152,125.00	13,052.81	$2,959,552.86	2,114.40	$529,236.34	281.68	15,448.89
WMD Total:	*5*	*0.00*	*$0.00*	*523.00*	*$410,400.00*	*44,199.83*	*$13,442,627.50*	*13,746.17*	*$3,231,429.49*	*1,266.36*	*59,212.36*
Fergus Falls WMD											
Douglas		-1.33	$0.00	0.00	$0.00	9,608.49	$2,875,443.20	6,181.79	$978,805.98	495.95	16,286.23
Grant		0.00	$0.00	106.50	$34,575.00	10,498.09	$3,992,838.12	3,861.39	$1,425,904.00	174.46	14,533.94
Otter Tail		6.29	$93,500.00	40.90	$51,032.00	22,083.86	$9,327,052.26	16,082.77	$5,184,512.25	184.29	38,350.92
Wilkin		0.00	$0.00	0.00	$0.00	2,433.26	$900,064.35	309.00	$93,750.00	75.10	2,817.36
WMD Total:	*4*	*4.96*	*$93,500.00*	*147.40*	*$85,607.00*	*44,623.70*	*$17,095,397.93*	*26,434.95*	*$7,682,972.23*	*929.80*	*71,988.45*
Litchfield WMD											
Aitkin		0.00	$0.00	0.00	$0.00	69.86	$28,000.00	0.00	$0.00	0.00	69.86
Kandiyohi		0.00	$0.00	0.00	$0.00	13,884.78	$6,515,218.93	4,718.73	$1,098,326.80	51.18	18,654.69
McLeod		0.00	$0.00	0.00	$0.00	1,720.79	$3,646,793.00	996.52	$984,644.90	0.00	2,717.31

Table 2. Waterfowl Production Areas

State and Unit		FISCAL YEAR MBCF ACQUISITION				CUMULATIVE TOTALS AT END OF FISCAL YEAR					
		Purchased		Easement or Lease		MBCF Purchased		Easement or Lease		All Other Acres	Total Acres
		Acres	Cost	Acres	Cost	Acres	Cost	Acres	Cost		
Minnesota (Continued)											
Litchfield WMD											
Meeker		0.00	$0.00	0.00	$0.00	4,866.29	$4,157,389.10	2,579.64	$1,344,142.00	0.61	7,446.54
Renville		0.00	$0.00	0.00	$0.00	1,658.03	$2,211,040.00	0.00	$0.00	0.00	1,658.03
Stearns		0.00	$0.00	0.00	$0.00	9,173.36	$3,023,333.87	1,602.81	$734,660.70	220.70	10,996.87
Todd		0.00	$0.00	0.00	$0.00	802.85	$385,672.20	42.58	$17,480.00	0.00	845.43
Wright		0.00	$0.00	0.00	$0.00	3,070.12	$6,276,520.90	437.50	$223,575.00	0.00	3,507.62
WMD Total:	8	*0.00*	*$0.00*	*0.00*	*$0.00*	*35,246.08*	*$26,243,968.00*	*10,377.78*	*$4,402,829.40*	*272.49*	*45,896.35*
Minnesota Valley WMD											
Blue Earth		0.00	$0.00	0.00	$0.00	1,182.77	$1,657,250.00	735.61	$1,156,550.00	138.37	2,056.75
Carver		0.00	$0.00	0.00	$0.00	0.00	$0.00	47.57	$68,976.50	219.00	266.57
Dakota		0.00	$0.00	0.00	$0.00	73.90	$201,747.00	0.00	$0.00	0.05	73.95
Lesueur		0.00	$0.00	0.00	$0.00	356.11	$525,754.50	242.15	$222,878.50	62.88	661.14
Rice		0.00	$0.00	0.00	$0.00	315.60	$438,999.35	580.79	$1,020,141.25	105.50	1,001.89
Scott		0.00	$0.00	0.00	$0.00	40.00	$109,200.00	164.21	$248,001.00	0.00	204.21
Sibley		0.00	$0.00	0.00	$0.00	793.52	$1,007,681.32	253.25	$173,190.00	112.36	1,159.13
Steele		0.00	$0.00	0.00	$0.00	650.11	$833,744.00	0.00	$0.00	16.59	666.70
Waseca		0.00	$0.00	0.00	$0.00	248.78	$408,000.00	0.00	$0.00	0.00	248.78
WMD Total:	9	*0.00*	*$0.00*	*0.00*	*$0.00*	*3,660.79*	*$5,182,376.17*	*2,023.58*	*$2,889,737.25*	*654.75*	*6,339.12*
Morris WMD											
Big Stone		0.00	$0.00	646.64	$785,725.00	11,534.74	$2,340,945.83	9,850.14	$3,315,831.16	201.37	21,586.25
Chippewa		0.00	$0.00	0.00	$0.00	244.10	$127,050.00	115.10	$105,525.00	0.00	359.20
Lac Qui Parle		0.00	$0.00	20.50	$35,925.00	3,808.79	$1,002,339.73	1,936.19	$914,191.00	278.63	6,023.61
Pope		0.00	$0.00	710.46	$785,400.00	13,120.49	$3,066,945.07	11,280.24	$3,317,386.70	80.00	24,480.73
Stevens		0.00	$0.00	0.00	$0.00	9,552.66	$3,463,001.64	1,234.50	$370,390.00	139.72	10,926.88
Swift		0.00	$0.00	0.00	$0.00	7,635.58	$1,860,080.17	2,127.67	$941,019.40	0.00	9,763.25
Traverse		0.00	$0.00	0.00	$0.00	4,105.55	$1,469,588.63	1,443.61	$307,665.00	0.00	5,549.16
Yellow Medicine		0.00	$0.00	243.38	$257,250.00	1,082.68	$879,683.30	1,113.77	$822,302.40	0.00	2,196.45
WMD Total:	8	*0.00*	*$0.00*	*1,620.98*	*$1,864,300.00*	*51,084.59*	*$14,209,634.37*	*29,101.22*	*$10,094,310.66*	*699.72*	*80,885.53*
Tamarac WMD											
Cass		0.00	$0.00	0.00	$0.00	0.00	$0.00	43.00	$6,000.00	0.00	43.00
Clearwater		0.00	$0.00	0.00	$0.00	0.00	$0.00	864.00	$129,075.00	0.00	864.00
WMD Total:	2	*0.00*	*$0.00*	*0.00*	*$0.00*	*0.00*	*$0.00*	*907.00*	*$135,075.00*	*0.00*	*907.00*
Windom WMD											
Cottonwood		0.00	$0.00	0.00	$0.00	3,137.96	$1,681,553.85	233.12	$132,625.00	0.00	3,371.08
Faribault		0.00	$0.00	0.00	$0.00	830.06	$800,991.80	129.37	$110,775.00	0.00	959.43
Freeborn		0.00	$0.00	0.00	$0.00	1,808.27	$2,373,017.25	147.99	$161,650.00	133.61	2,089.87
Jackson		-0.27	$0.00	40.00	$95,325.00	4,694.97	$4,497,146.28	423.09	$642,725.00	0.00	5,118.06
Martin		0.00	$0.00	0.00	$0.00	333.89	$645,369.60	271.65	$287,184.39	0.00	605.54
Mower		0.00	$0.00	0.00	$0.00	0.00	$0.00	0.00	$0.00	99.64	99.64
Murray		0.00	$0.00	0.00	$0.00	2,221.94	$2,691,477.00	31.86	$57,875.00	0.00	2,253.80
Nobles		0.00	$0.00	0.00	$0.00	521.65	$580,802.00	26.00	$15,600.00	0.00	547.65
Rock		0.00	$0.00	0.00	$0.00	0.00	$0.00	104.79	$233,950.00	0.00	104.79
Watonwan		0.00	$0.00	0.00	$0.00	56.65	$31,157.50	168.42	$112,209.80	0.00	225.07
WMD Total:	9	*-0.27*	*$0.00*	*40.00*	*$95,325.00*	*13,605.39*	*$13,301,515.28*	*1,536.29*	*$1,754,594.19*	*233.25*	*15,374.93*
State Total	48	**4.69**	**$93,500.00**	**2,479.50**	**$2,669,007.00**	**195,305.61**	**$92,363,939.25**	**86,299.32**	**$31,701,399.26**	**4,056.37**	**285,661.30**
Montana											
Benton Lake WMD											
Cascade		0.00	$0.00	0.00	$0.00	727.46	$299,606.00	78.00	$15,550.00	193.50	998.96
Chouteau		0.00	$0.00	0.00	$822.36	2,136.13	$538,543.00	661.00	$28,671.43	280.00	3,077.13
Glacier		0.00	$0.00	0.00	$0.00	94.20	$17,898.00	10,146.83	$953,495.00	96.50	10,337.53
Hill		0.00	$0.00	0.00	$1,332.00	0.00	$0.00	918.00	$89,937.00	378.93	1,296.93
Lewis and Clark		0.00	$0.00	0.00	$0.00	0.00	$0.00	3,317.07	$1,071,782.00	2,810.88	6,127.95
Liberty		0.00	$0.00	0.00	$0.00	0.00	$0.00	428.00	$14,100.00	0.00	428.00
Pondera		0.00	$0.00	0.00	$0.00	640.00	$93,000.00	8,715.01	$1,990,000.00	94.96	9,449.97
Powell		0.00	$0.00	0.00	$0.00	1,607.60	$811,084.00	23,203.06	$6,650,635.00	4,807.60	29,618.26
Teton	*	0.00	$0.00	0.00	$0.00	1,486.05	$376,253.00	5,413.13	$241,818.00	921.64	7,820.82

Table 2. Waterfowl Production Areas

State and Unit		FISCAL YEAR MBCF ACQUISITION				CUMULATIVE TOTALS AT END OF FISCAL YEAR					
		Purchased		Easement or Lease		MBCF				All Other Acres	Total Acres
						Purchased		Easement or Lease			
		Acres	Cost	Acres	Cost	Acres	Cost	Acres	Cost		
Montana (Continued)											
Benton Lake WMD											
Toole		0.00	$0.00	0.00	$0.00	4,610.48	$1,003,964.00	12,161.09	$916,245.00	5.28	16,776.85
WMD Total:	10	0.00	$0.00	0.00	$2,154.36	11,301.92	$3,140,348.00	65,041.19	$11,972,233.43	9,589.29	85,932.40
Bowdoin WMD											
Blaine		0.00	$0.00	0.00	$0.00	2,435.26	$167,340.00	7,783.93	$896,395.00	11,783.00	22,002.19
Phillips	*	0.00	$0.00	1,926.50	$420,048.24	7,017.35	$1,476,863.00	36,450.77	$3,171,771.18	11,451.71	54,919.83
Valley		0.00	$0.00	0.00	$0.00	0.00	$0.00	201.00	$28,160.00	0.00	201.00
WMD Total:	3	0.00	$0.00	1,926.50	$420,048.24	9,452.61	$1,644,203.00	44,435.70	$4,096,326.18	23,234.71	77,123.02
Charles M. Russell WMD											
Golden Valley		0.00	$0.00	0.00	$211.82	760.27	$76,427.00	160.00	$6,858.55	0.00	920.27
Musselshell		0.00	$0.00	0.00	$864.00	532.45	$163,001.00	160.00	$12,683.00	0.00	692.45
Petroleum		0.00	$0.00	0.00	$0.00	40.00	$23,800.00	0.00	$0.00	0.00	40.00
Stillwater		0.00	$0.00	0.00	$0.00	1,828.10	$207,625.00	0.00	$0.00	0.38	1,828.48
Yellowstone		0.00	$0.00	0.00	$0.00	486.42	$55,600.00	0.00	$0.00	0.00	486.42
WMD Total:	5	0.00	$0.00	0.00	$1,075.82	3,647.24	$526,453.00	320.00	$19,541.55	0.38	3,967.62
NE Montana WMD											
Daniels		0.00	$0.00	0.00	$0.00	1,080.58	$97,669.00	472.65	$41,125.00	546.52	2,099.75
Roosevelt		0.00	$0.00	0.00	$0.00	179.20	$14,000.00	7,402.42	$392,500.00	0.00	7,581.62
Sheridan		0.00	$0.00	0.00	$0.00	9,328.01	$950,442.23	10,030.20	$699,025.00	2,677.13	22,035.34
WMD Total:	3	0.00	$0.00	0.00	$0.00	10,587.79	$1,062,111.23	17,905.27	$1,132,650.00	3,223.65	31,716.71
NW Montana - Flathead WMD											
Flathead		0.00	$0.00	0.00	$0.00	4,410.31	$2,246,518.00	0.00	$0.00	807.92	5,218.23
WMD Total:	1	0.00	$0.00	0.00	$0.00	4,410.31	$2,246,518.00	0.00	$0.00	807.92	5,218.23
NW Montana - Lake WMD											
Lake	*	0.00	$0.00	0.00	$0.00	1,480.86	$1,460,555.00	4,131.61	$3,103,430.00	1,949.14	7,561.61
WMD Total:	1	0.00	$0.00	0.00	$0.00	1,480.86	$1,460,555.00	4,131.61	$3,103,430.00	1,949.14	7,561.61
State Total	23	0.00	$0.00	1,926.50	$423,278.42	40,880.73	$10,080,188.23	131,833.77	$20,324,181.16	38,805.09	211,519.59
Nebraska											
Rainwater Basin WMD											
Adams		0.00	$0.00	0.00	$0.00	160.00	$110,000.00	0.00	$11,316.89	234.56	394.56
Clay		0.00	$0.00	0.88	$0.00	4,216.27	$1,622,444.00	0.88	$0.00	2,833.78	7,050.93
Fillmore		0.00	$0.00	0.00	$0.00	2,937.60	$1,142,453.00	6.60	$24.00	638.90	3,583.10
Franklin		0.00	$0.00	0.00	$0.00	1,625.96	$402,698.00	0.00	$0.00	157.36	1,783.32
Gosper		0.00	$0.00	0.00	$0.00	1,451.50	$233,923.00	0.00	$0.00	0.00	1,451.50
Hall	*	0.00	$0.00	0.00	$0.00	328.77	$433,000.00	0.00	$0.00	320.70	649.47
Hamilton	*	0.00	$0.00	0.00	$0.00	400.00	$407,450.00	0.00	$5,899.02	785.17	1,185.17
Kearney	*	0.00	$0.00	0.00	$0.00	2,874.43	$657,681.00	0.00	$0.00	253.98	3,128.41
Phelps		0.00	$0.00	0.00	$0.00	4,195.14	$3,052,111.00	0.00	$0.00	400.00	4,595.14
Polk FSA	**	0.00	$0.00	0.00	$0.00	0.00	$0.00	0.00	$0.00	140.78	140.78
Saline FSA	**	0.00	$0.00	0.00	$0.00	0.00	$0.00	0.00	$0.00	104.35	104.35
Seward		-2.16	$0.00	0.00	$0.00	278.67	$101,746.45	0.00	$0.00	342.31	620.98
York	*	0.00	$0.00	0.00	$0.00	679.20	$194,429.00	0.00	$0.00	372.86	1,052.06
WMD Total:	11	-2.16	$0.00	0.88	$0.00	19,147.54	$8,357,935.45	7.48	$17,239.91	6,584.75	25,739.77
State Total	11	-2.16	$0.00	0.88	$0.00	19,147.54	$8,357,935.45	7.48	$17,239.91	6,584.75	25,739.77
North Dakota											
Arrowwood WMD											
Eddy	*	0.00	$0.00	0.00	$0.00	4,627.21	$498,001.00	11,810.63	$314,995.00	446.34	16,884.18
Foster		0.00	$0.00	0.00	$0.00	1,487.07	$96,568.00	6,946.00	$239,015.00	0.00	8,433.07
WMD Total:	2	0.00	$0.00	0.00	$0.00	6,114.28	$594,569.00	18,756.63	$554,010.00	446.34	25,317.25
Audubon WMD											
Hettinger		0.00	$0.00	0.00	$0.00	0.00	$0.00	0.00	$0.00	1,202.60	1,202.60
McLean		0.00	$0.00	101.00	$35,075.00	4,219.10	$536,234.00	23,071.00	$1,572,990.00	21,821.61	49,111.71
Sheridan	*	0.00	$0.00	1,030.75	$239,400.00	7,661.50	$468,427.00	33,999.34	$1,783,520.00	30,488.34	72,149.18
Ward		0.00	$0.00	0.00	$0.00	5,868.60	$489,211.00	38,909.61	$1,416,814.00	13,218.97	57,997.18
WMD Total:	4	0.00	$0.00	1,131.75	$274,475.00	17,749.20	$1,493,872.00	95,979.95	$4,773,324.00	66,731.52	180,460.67

Table 2. Waterfowl Production Areas

State and Unit		FISCAL YEAR MBCF ACQUISITION				CUMULATIVE TOTALS AT END OF FISCAL YEAR					
		Purchased		Easement or Lease		MBCF				All Other Acres	Total Acres
						Purchased		Easement or Lease			
		Acres	Cost	Acres	Cost	Acres	Cost	Acres	Cost		
North Dakota (Continued)											
Chase Lake Prairie Project WMD											
Stutsman	*	0.00	$0.00	323.00	$77,050.00	23,403.35	$1,308,016.00	45,717.99	$1,674,740.00	34,202.20	103,323.54
Wells	*	0.00	$0.00	20.00	$6,700.00	7,471.61	$1,153,059.00	13,795.00	$738,202.00	6,386.02	27,652.63
WMD Total:	2	0.00	$0.00	343.00	$83,750.00	30,874.96	$2,461,075.00	59,512.99	$2,412,942.00	40,588.22	130,976.17
Crosby WMD											
Burke		0.00	$0.00	107.00	$28,200.00	3,545.96	$180,068.00	26,804.00	$721,580.00	19,826.66	50,176.62
Divide		0.00	$0.00	170.00	$26,225.00	9,444.62	$474,790.00	35,405.09	$742,460.00	7,913.93	52,763.64
Williams	*	0.00	$0.00	160.00	$33,500.00	4,163.17	$278,057.00	8,524.00	$255,625.00	1,561.32	14,248.49
WMD Total:	3	0.00	$0.00	437.00	$87,925.00	17,153.75	$932,915.00	70,733.09	$1,719,665.00	29,301.91	117,188.75
Devils Lake WMD											
Benson	*	0.00	$0.00	95.79	$34,325.00	7,296.77	$607,908.00	35,866.81	$1,081,655.00	8,423.55	51,587.13
Cavalier	*	0.00	$0.00	206.00	$81,250.00	10,129.12	$1,354,471.00	13,920.00	$403,040.00	1,272.71	25,321.83
Grand Forks		0.00	$0.00	0.00	$0.00	6,774.43	$1,594,422.05	1,118.00	$46,485.00	641.26	8,533.69
Nelson	*	0.00	$0.00	0.00	$0.00	3,203.23	$174,341.00	37,856.70	$1,336,445.00	2,753.12	43,813.05
Pembina	*	0.00	$0.00	0.00	$0.00	2,258.56	$218,677.00	139.00	$1,900.00	293.90	2,691.46
Ramsey	*	0.00	$0.00	0.00	$0.00	8,183.04	$1,144,252.00	29,524.00	$1,041,285.00	2,038.49	39,745.53
Towner	*	0.00	$0.00	0.00	$0.00	3,837.02	$494,146.00	24,361.40	$508,990.00	6,440.83	34,639.25
Walsh	*	0.00	$0.00	0.00	$0.00	1,393.19	$98,128.00	8,255.00	$118,800.00	1,234.63	10,882.82
WMD Total:	8	0.00	$0.00	301.79	$115,575.00	43,075.36	$5,686,345.05	151,040.91	$4,538,600.00	23,098.49	217,214.76
J. Clark Salyer WMD											
Bottineau	*	0.00	$0.00	35.00	$22,275.00	2,334.06	$200,763.00	30,368.69	$1,758,930.00	1,305.00	34,007.75
Mchenry	*	0.00	$0.00	0.00	$0.00	4,888.80	$374,404.50	31,954.00	$1,308,245.00	31,991.59	68,834.39
Pierce	*	7.40	$14,800.00	225.00	$81,050.00	8,403.66	$936,855.00	37,684.00	$1,518,060.00	11,552.87	57,640.53
Renville		0.00	$0.00	0.00	$0.00	311.09	$23,523.00	16,967.00	$1,841,665.00	31.60	17,309.69
Rolette		0.00	$0.00	460.00	$128,325.00	5,685.92	$759,347.00	20,667.01	$613,695.00	722.96	27,075.89
WMD Total:	5	7.40	$14,800.00	720.00	$231,650.00	21,623.53	$2,294,892.50	137,640.70	$7,040,595.00	45,604.02	204,868.25
Kulm WMD											
Dickey	*	0.00	$0.00	20.00	$4,900.00	9,735.40	$1,150,816.00	29,025.80	$1,851,075.00	16,810.71	55,571.91
La Moure	*	0.00	$0.00	126.00	$74,125.00	4,799.96	$505,095.00	14,716.25	$1,220,174.00	2,629.31	22,145.52
Logan	*	0.00	$0.00	14.00	$2,525.00	11,226.24	$1,006,598.00	39,365.50	$1,261,336.00	21,759.00	72,350.74
Mcintosh	*	0.00	$0.00	0.00	$0.00	17,373.48	$1,368,865.00	30,821.00	$889,985.00	11,239.28	59,433.76
WMD Total:	4	0.00	$0.00	160.00	$81,550.00	43,135.08	$4,031,374.00	113,928.55	$5,222,570.00	52,438.30	209,501.93
Long Lake WMD											
Burleigh	*	0.00	$0.00	177.00	$69,025.00	9,451.44	$1,899,164.00	27,742.10	$919,375.00	36,922.17	74,115.71
Emmons	*	0.00	$0.00	610.00	$111,675.00	3,135.29	$174,321.75	12,593.00	$479,450.00	3,827.81	19,556.10
Kidder	*	0.00	$0.00	0.00	$0.00	5,547.52	$438,439.00	65,066.02	$1,109,380.00	45,522.60	116,136.14
WMD Total:	3	0.00	$0.00	787.00	$180,700.00	18,134.25	$2,511,924.75	105,401.12	$2,508,205.00	86,272.58	209,807.95
Lostwood WMD											
Mountrail	*	0.00	$0.00	0.00	$0.00	9,905.10	$940,661.00	31,898.00	$991,856.00	37,721.28	79,524.38
WMD Total:	1	0.00	$0.00	0.00	$0.00	9,905.10	$940,661.00	31,898.00	$991,856.00	37,721.28	79,524.38
Tewaukon WMD											
Ransom		0.00	$0.00	104.48	$102,825.00	4,315.02	$617,357.00	20,831.08	$1,716,475.00	3,959.58	29,105.68
Richland		0.00	$0.00	88.00	$36,275.00	6,072.25	$986,052.00	2,261.80	$427,620.00	4,886.32	13,220.37
Sargent	*	0.00	$0.00	-5.00	$0.00	3,537.46	$305,439.00	14,592.40	$1,002,610.00	10,021.45	28,151.31
WMD Total:	3	0.00	$0.00	187.48	$139,100.00	13,924.73	$1,908,848.00	37,685.28	$3,146,705.00	18,867.35	70,477.36
Valley City WMD											
Barnes	*	0.00	$0.00	404.00	$371,425.00	6,661.68	$958,087.00	20,077.00	$2,281,035.00	2,347.51	29,086.19
Cass		0.00	$0.00	0.00	$0.00	3,439.89	$628,344.00	1,709.00	$133,825.00	50.90	5,199.79
Griggs		0.00	$0.00	0.00	$0.00	3,069.46	$373,990.00	16,677.00	$536,830.00	259.25	20,005.71
Steele		0.00	$0.00	0.00	$0.00	3,249.25	$538,345.00	4,045.00	$274,320.00	359.30	7,653.55
Traill		0.00	$0.00	0.00	$0.00	719.36	$75,109.00	233.00	$4,830.00	1.00	953.36
WMD Total:	5	0.00	$0.00	404.00	$371,425.00	17,139.64	$2,573,875.00	42,741.00	$3,230,840.00	3,017.96	62,898.60
State Total	40	7.40	$14,800.00	4,472.02	$1,566,150.00	238,829.88	$25,430,351.30	865,318.22	$36,139,312.00	404,087.97	1,508,236.07
South Dakota											
Huron WMD											
Beadle	*	0.00	$0.00	310.00	$186,445.00	7,256.45	$1,651,212.69	45,661.95	$8,394,640.00	1,892.59	54,810.99

Table 2. Waterfowl Production Areas

		FISCAL YEAR MBCF ACQUISITION			CUMULATIVE TOTALS AT END OF FISCAL YEAR					
					MBCF				All Other Acres	Total Acres
		Purchased		Easement or Lease		Purchased		Easement or Lease		
State and Unit		Acres	Cost	Acres	Cost	Acres	Cost	Acres	Cost	Acres	Acres
South Dakota (Continued)											
Huron WMD											
Buffalo		0.00	$0.00	733.45	$199,428.00	0.00	$0.00	2,631.06	$478,453.00	6,393.23	9,024.29
Hand	*	0.00	$0.00	0.00	$0.00	3,670.56	$580,260.35	64,301.90	$9,087,424.00	5,953.88	73,926.34
Hughes		0.00	$0.00	0.00	$0.00	455.99	$82,800.00	3,260.89	$444,875.00	4.20	3,721.08
Hyde	*	0.00	$0.00	0.00	$0.00	0.00	$0.00	32,129.34	$3,110,385.00	12,376.82	44,506.16
Jerauld	*	0.00	$0.00	421.40	$164,500.00	1,430.40	$217,041.00	25,439.72	$3,154,040.00	894.70	27,764.82
Sanborn	*	0.00	$0.00	1,663.88	$945,225.00	93.00	$5,250.00	43,048.79	$7,337,245.00	568.20	43,709.99
Sully	*	0.00	$0.00	0.00	$0.00	266.48	$9,993.00	4,072.73	$626,590.00	1,983.48	6,322.69
WMD Total:	8	0.00	$0.00	3,128.73	$1,495,598.00	13,172.88	$2,546,557.04	220,546.38	$32,633,652.00	30,067.10	263,786.36
Lacreek WMD											
Haakon FSA	**	0.00	$0.00	0.00	$0.00	0.00	$0.00	0.00	$0.00	1,806.10	1,806.10
Jones FSA	**	0.00	$0.00	0.00	$0.00	0.00	$0.00	0.00	$0.00	221.97	221.97
Stanley FSA	**	0.00	$0.00	0.00	$0.00	0.00	$0.00	0.00	$0.00	1,430.30	1,430.30
WMD Total:	0	0.00	$0.00	0.00	$0.00	0.00	$0.00	0.00	$0.00	3,458.37	3,458.37
Lake Andes WMD											
Aurora	*	0.00	$0.00	0.00	$0.00	4,876.08	$798,316.00	40,774.05	$7,680,470.00	495.90	46,146.03
Bon Homme	*	0.00	$0.00	244.00	$212,825.00	1,174.17	$323,624.90	403.00	$217,130.00	323.54	1,900.71
Brule		0.00	$0.00	198.86	$91,800.00	1,074.13	$89,404.00	21,432.74	$3,473,005.00	866.26	23,373.13
Charles Mix	*	0.00	$0.00	68.00	$68,350.00	4,110.82	$1,162,147.00	8,988.41	$1,819,935.00	1,396.31	14,495.54
Clay	*	0.00	$0.00	0.00	$0.00	40.00	$8,000.00	7.00	$200.00	52.50	99.50
Davison	*	0.00	$0.00	0.00	$0.00	229.92	$24,540.00	778.67	$415,465.00	175.10	1,183.69
Douglas	*	0.00	$0.00	0.00	$0.00	3,852.05	$647,691.00	4,093.28	$521,450.00	619.27	8,564.60
Hanson	*	0.00	$0.00	222.00	$233,750.00	1,075.60	$281,853.00	3,402.01	$878,780.00	132.80	4,610.41
Hutchinson	*	0.00	$0.00	0.00	$0.00	789.51	$227,646.25	1,057.00	$151,075.00	172.50	2,019.01
Lincoln		0.00	$0.00	0.00	$0.00	177.22	$39,925.00	300.50	$112,645.00	0.00	477.72
Tripp FSA	**	0.00	$0.00	0.00	$0.00	0.00	$0.00	0.00	$0.00	5.90	5.90
Turner	*	0.00	$0.00	0.00	$0.00	991.73	$727,444.90	353.00	$106,090.00	126.90	1,471.63
Union		0.00	$0.00	0.00	$0.00	96.02	$22,331.00	0.00	$0.00	0.00	96.02
Yankton		0.00	$0.00	0.00	$0.00	294.63	$128,562.00	123.00	$5,375.00	365.60	783.23
WMD Total:	13	0.00	$0.00	732.86	$606,725.00	18,781.88	$4,481,485.05	81,712.66	$15,381,620.00	4,732.58	105,227.12
Madison WMD											
Brookings	*	0.00	$0.00	39.00	$27,550.00	6,159.47	$1,650,276.70	7,976.05	$2,188,866.00	4,010.37	18,145.89
Deuel	*	0.00	$0.00	363.00	$164,225.00	3,228.87	$492,022.00	28,701.29	$4,019,200.00	7,113.48	39,043.64
Hamlin	*	0.00	$0.00	47.50	$59,500.00	3,375.89	$943,938.00	6,242.74	$1,130,630.00	323.90	9,942.53
Kingsbury	*	0.00	$0.00	436.49	$347,125.00	5,256.36	$1,258,255.50	25,569.20	$4,040,353.00	4,679.00	35,504.56
Lake	*	0.00	$0.00	113.00	$167,100.00	5,672.95	$1,296,457.75	6,657.32	$1,953,635.00	917.12	13,247.39
McCook	*	0.00	$0.00	41.06	$30,425.00	3,362.96	$680,845.60	6,911.31	$1,379,645.00	835.37	11,109.64
Miner	*	0.00	$0.00	1,448.23	$1,054,100.00	1,545.87	$153,695.00	26,818.15	$7,712,390.00	1,299.80	29,663.82
Minnehaha	*	0.00	$0.00	0.00	$0.00	4,606.03	$1,342,286.00	1,720.44	$387,620.00	27.60	6,354.07
Moody	*	0.00	$0.00	0.00	$0.00	2,903.78	$927,478.85	1,959.02	$645,930.00	705.89	5,568.69
WMD Total:	9	0.00	$0.00	2,488.28	$1,850,025.00	36,112.18	$8,745,255.40	112,555.52	$23,458,269.00	19,912.53	168,580.23
Sand Lake WMD											
Brown		0.00	$0.00	368.71	$249,750.00	4,094.93	$819,223.80	51,740.28	$7,322,650.00	1,444.49	57,279.70
Campbell		0.00	$0.00	0.00	$0.00	1,919.71	$185,541.00	26,328.51	$2,389,605.00	526.20	28,774.42
Corson FSA	**	0.00	$0.00	0.00	$0.00	0.00	$0.00	0.00	$0.00	1,105.90	1,105.90
Dewey FSA	**	0.00	$0.00	0.00	$0.00	0.00	$0.00	0.00	$0.00	2,361.80	2,361.80
Edmunds	*	72.10	$50,000.00	164.94	$72,425.00	9,037.86	$1,767,201.00	132,538.23	$14,275,185.00	2,692.47	144,268.56
Faulk	*	0.00	$0.00	86.00	$54,925.00	2,566.88	$480,995.00	137,992.93	$11,411,090.00	3,721.36	144,281.17
Mcpherson	*	0.00	$0.00	849.47	$288,225.00	19,254.66	$3,375,636.80	146,735.00	$9,088,890.00	12,927.53	178,917.19
Potter	*	0.00	$0.00	0.00	$0.00	652.63	$71,179.00	26,372.60	$2,030,680.00	415.10	27,440.33
Spink	*	0.00	$0.00	0.00	$0.00	2,233.86	$399,130.00	29,150.55	$4,311,000.00	1,308.20	32,692.61
Walworth	*	0.00	$0.00	35.00	$14,450.00	1,524.54	$191,800.00	21,417.44	$1,894,090.00	853.30	23,795.28
WMD Total:	8	72.10	$50,000.00	1,504.12	$679,775.00	41,285.07	$7,290,706.60	572,275.54	$52,723,190.00	27,356.35	640,916.96
Waubay WMD											
Clark	*	0.00	$0.00	346.42	$126,725.00	5,873.11	$814,503.90	46,155.28	$3,109,450.00	1,186.43	53,214.82
Codington	*	0.00	$0.00	388.52	$175,000.00	5,089.31	$882,837.70	11,117.17	$942,515.00	1,566.65	17,773.13

Table 2. Waterfowl Production Areas

State and Unit		FISCAL YEAR MBCF ACQUISITION				CUMULATIVE TOTALS AT END OF FISCAL YEAR					
		Purchased		Easement or Lease		MBCF				All Other Acres	Total Acres
						Purchased		Easement or Lease			
		Acres	Cost	Acres	Cost	Acres	Cost	Acres	Cost	Acres	Acres
South Dakota (Continued)											
Waubay WMD											
Day		208.64	$350,000.00	330.64	$147,275.00	6,541.27	$807,107.00	45,309.19	$3,345,045.00	1,653.75	53,504.21
Grant		0.00	$0.00	734.02	$457,850.00	5,362.99	$1,005,000.00	24,045.19	$3,693,360.00	437.85	29,846.03
Marshall	*	0.00	$0.00	236.56	$117,050.00	10,098.51	$1,923,929.00	58,494.91	$4,697,731.00	966.90	69,560.32
Roberts	*	0.00	$0.00	506.42	$150,075.00	5,150.73	$823,410.80	51,689.17	$3,776,475.00	2,728.08	59,567.98
WMD Total:	6	208.64	$350,000.00	2,542.58	$1,173,975.00	38,115.92	$6,256,788.40	236,810.91	$19,564,576.00	8,539.66	283,466.49
State Total	44	280.74	$400,000.00	10,396.57	$5,806,098.00	147,467.93	$29,320,792.49	1,223,901.01	$143,761,307.00	94,066.59	1,465,435.53
Wisconsin											
Leopold WMD											
Adams		0.00	$0.00	0.00	$0.00	344.00	$172,500.00	0.00	$0.00	0.00	344.00
Columbia		22.09	$175,000.00	0.00	$0.00	3,663.33	$5,022,951.45	0.00	$0.00	66.85	3,730.18
Dane		135.78	$1,020,000.00	0.00	$0.00	1,671.36	$2,979,875.65	0.00	$0.00	55.50	1,726.86
Dodge		0.00	$0.00	0.00	$0.00	698.98	$1,079,141.16	0.43	$1,000.00	109.81	809.22
Fond Du Lac		204.50	$818,000.00	0.00	$0.00	881.06	$1,699,888.00	0.00	$0.00	284.84	1,165.90
Jefferson		0.00	$0.00	0.00	$0.00	249.79	$241,239.00	0.00	$0.00	0.00	249.79
Manitowoc		0.00	$0.00	0.00	$0.00	256.13	$186,000.00	0.00	$0.00	0.00	256.13
Marquette		0.00	$0.00	0.00	$0.00	259.97	$119,480.00	0.00	$0.00	0.00	259.97
Ozaukee		0.00	$0.00	0.00	$0.00	709.30	$1,591,413.40	0.00	$0.00	0.00	709.30
Rock		0.00	$0.00	0.00	$0.00	349.32	$302,358.71	0.00	$0.00	0.00	349.32
Sauk		0.00	$0.00	0.00	$0.00	24.16	$136,000.00	0.00	$0.00	210.88	235.04
Sheboygan		0.00	$0.00	0.00	$0.00	485.92	$1,322,636.94	0.00	$0.00	223.99	709.91
Waushara		0.00	$0.00	0.00	$0.00	232.30	$243,000.00	0.00	$6,000.00	0.00	232.30
Winnebago		0.00	$0.00	0.00	$0.00	1,870.13	$1,348,651.00	0.00	$0.00	249.24	2,119.37
WMD Total:	14	362.37	$2,013,000.00	0.00	$0.00	11,695.75	$16,445,135.31	0.43	$7,000.00	1,201.11	12,897.29
St. Croix WMD											
Dunn		60.27	$178,500.00	0.00	$0.00	531.45	$680,700.00	0.00	$0.00	150.80	682.25
Polk		0.00	$0.00	0.00	$0.00	845.09	$417,424.00	0.00	$0.00	221.98	1,067.07
St. Croix		0.00	$0.00	0.00	$0.00	5,519.75	$8,209,039.56	0.64	$1,500.00	260.41	5,780.80
WMD Total:	3	60.27	$178,500.00	0.00	$0.00	6,896.29	$9,307,163.56	0.64	$1,500.00	633.19	7,530.12
State Total	17	422.64	$2,191,500.00	0.00	$0.00	18,592.04	$25,752,298.87	1.07	$8,500.00	1,834.30	20,427.41
Grand Total	206	987.51	$3,974,100.00	19,275.47	$10,464,533.42	687,382.91	$232,772,493.41	2,307,832.57	$232,374,264.33	550,574.78	3,545,790.26

* These counties include interests transferred by the FSA.
** Denotes interests transferred by the FSA.

FSA - Farm Service Agency (Formerly Farmers Home Administration, Department of Agriculture)

North American Wetlands Conservation Fund (NAWCF)

Summary of MBCC Approvals for Fiscal Year 2011

The Migratory Bird Conservation Commission approved 64 wetland conservation project proposals for funding in Fiscal Year 2011 under the North American Wetlands Conservation Act. A total of $75,835,580 from the North American Wetlands Conservation Fund, together with $217,231,148 in partner funds, are supporting 50 projects in the United States, 6 in Canada, and 8 in Mexico. The following tables provide summary and detailed project information.

Fiscal Year 2011

Projects Approved by the Migratory Bird Conservation Commission and Active Under the North American Wetlands Conservation Act

Country	No. of Projects	Act Funds	Partner Funds	Acres Affected
U.S.	50	$49,306,106	$163,938,653	235,355
Canada	6	$23,559,250	$33,893,685	139,725
Mexico	8	$2,970,224	$19,398,810	277,213
Total	64	$75,835,580	$217,231,148	652,293
U.S. Small Grants	*45*	*$3,167,794*	*$21,128,732*	*25,017*

In addition, the Commission approved 45 United States small grant proposals, totaling $3,167,794 from the Fund, supported by $21,128,732 in partner funds, affecting 25,017 acres.

PINTAIL

Table 3. U.S. Wetlands Conservation Standard Grants Proposals

Project Name	State Province	NAWCA Grant	Non-Fed Match	Non-Fed Non-Match	Federal Funds	Total Partners	Total Cost	Total Acres
ACADIA ARCHIPELAGO	ME	$1,000,000	$4,450,000	$0	$0	$4,450,000	$5,450,000	1,101
ACE BASIN: EDISTO RIVER CORRIDOR V	SC	$979,320	$11,934,400	$0	$0	$11,934,400	$12,913,720	2,220
ARK-LA-MISS WETLANDS CONSERVATION II	AR,LA	$999,917	$1,944,675	$0	$108,367	$2,053,042	$3,052,959	1,753
AUSTIN'S WOODS IV	TX	$1,000,000	$2,854,000	$130,000	$50,000	$3,034,000	$4,034,000	1,113
BIG OXBOW WETLAND ACQUISITION, PHASE II	ND	$282,539	$282,739	$0	$0	$282,739	$565,278	481
BUZZARDS BAY: LITTLE RIVER	MA	$925,025	$4,240,000	$0	$0	$4,240,000	$5,165,025	134
BUZZARDS BAY: LOWER WEWEANTIC	MA	$796,306	$806,100	$0	$0	$806,100	$1,602,406	128
CARTERET COUNTY, NC COASTAL INITIATIVE	NC	$1,000,000	$2,028,000	$0	$1,426,000	$3,454,000	$4,454,000	1,105
CHELSEA CREEK WETLANDS AND HABITAT CONSERVATION PROJECT	MA	$1,663,150	$5,604,100	$0	$0	$5,604,100	$7,267,250	17
COASTAL MARIN WETLANDS RESTORATION PROJECT II	CA	$998,900	$1,998,852	$0	$542,100	$2,540,952	$3,539,852	552
COBSCOOK BAY, BOLD COAST PROJECT AREA PHASE II	ME	$1,000,000	$2,187,240	$0	$15,000	$2,202,240	$3,202,240	974
CONSERVATION IN THE CONFLUENCE II	MO	$997,755	$2,866,937	$0	$0	$2,866,937	$3,864,692	1,181
DEADWATER, NECHES RIVER NWR	TX	$1,000,000	$2,255,000	$0	$101,847	$2,356,847	$3,356,847	2,090
DELAWARE BAYSHORES LAND PROTECTION AND CLIMATE CHANGE ADAPTATION	DE	$900,000	$2,501,456	$0	$0	$2,501,456	$3,401,456	664
DOS RIOS RANCH	CA	$1,000,000	$7,059,497	$0	$0	$7,059,497	$8,059,497	757
GLACIAL RIDGE PRAIRIE LANDSCAPE EXPANSION	MN	$1,000,000	$2,482,689	$0	$0	$2,482,689	$3,482,689	4,288
GLACIATED WETLANDS AND PRAIRIES OF ND AND MN	MN,ND	$1,000,000	$1,038,172	$0	$30,825	$1,068,997	$2,068,997	11,717
GREAT MARSH HABITAT PROTECTION	MA	$1,000,000	$2,116,000	$0	$0	$2,116,000	$3,116,000	210
GULF COAST WETLANDS RESTORATION AND ENHANCEMENT III	LA,TX	$1,000,000	$2,140,533	$0	$28,172	$2,168,705	$3,168,705	6,822
HARVEY DUNN GRASSLAND PRESERVATION PROJECT, IV	SD	$1,000,000	$1,064,527	$0	$0	$1,064,527	$2,064,527	2,397
HENRY'S FORK III	ID	$1,000,000	$2,015,910	$0	$0	$2,015,910	$3,015,910	2,030
KLAMATH BASIN WETLANDS II	CA	$1,000,000	$2,063,939	$0	$186,284	$2,250,223	$3,250,223	11,515
LAKE ONTARIO WATERSHED AND COASTAL WETLAND PROTECTION: PHASE I	NY	$1,000,000	$2,000,000	$7,793,502	$0	$9,793,502	$10,793,502	7,162
LIVING FLOODPLAINS OF NW OREGON AND SW WASHINGTON, PHASE II	OR	$1,000,000	$2,012,086	$0	$0	$2,012,086	$3,012,086	762
LIVING FLOODPLAINS OF NW OREGON AND SW WASHINGTON, PHASE III	OR	$1,000,000	$2,065,551	$0	$0	$2,065,551	$3,065,551	725
LOWER YELLOWSTONE WETLANDS CONSERVATION PROJECT, PHASE I	MT	$785,951	$1,705,439	$0	$99,300	$1,804,739	$2,590,690	3,006
MISSOURI COTEAU HABITAT CONSERVATION PROJECT, IX	ND	$1,000,000	$1,078,976	$0	$0	$1,078,976	$2,078,976	16,138
MUKWONAGO, FOX RIVER WATERSHED INITIATIVE	WI	$1,000,000	$5,911,586	$0	$0	$5,911,586	$6,911,586	4,153
NORTH DAKOTA NORTHERN PRAIRIE PROJECT	ND	$1,000,000	$1,072,016	$0	$150,409	$1,222,425	$2,222,425	55,253
NORTH PARK WETLAND CONSERVATION PARTNERSHIP	CO	$997,360	$4,350,042	$0	$62,857	$4,412,899	$5,410,259	8,367
NORTHEASTERN CALIFORNIA WETLANDS HABITAT PROJECT, PHASE I	CA	$1,000,000	$1,057,850	$0	$98,000	$1,155,850	$2,155,850	4,535
PISCATAQUIS RIVER / ALDER STREAM WETLANDS, PHASE II	ME	$1,000,000	$2,115,000	$16,600	$6,300	$2,137,900	$3,137,900	6,049
PLATTE RIVER CONFLUENCE PHASE III	NE	$997,038	$2,170,535	$0	$20,000	$2,190,535	$3,187,573	1,889
PLATTE RIVER WETLANDS PARTNERSHIP III	CO,WY	$999,945	$2,098,132	$0	$0	$2,098,132	$3,098,077	6,427
PRAIRIE LAKES V WETLAND INITIATIVE	IA	$1,000,000	$2,442,917	$0	$0	$2,442,917	$3,442,917	3,466
PRAIRIES WITHOUT BORDERS (PHASE II)	MN,ND,SD	$1,000,000	$1,002,300	$0	$58,300	$1,060,600	$2,060,600	2,630
ROCKY MOUNTAIN FRONT PROTECTION PROJECT III	MT	$1,000,000	$4,974,000	$0	$4,310,000	$9,284,000	$10,284,000	20,745
SAN LUIS VALLEY RIO GRANDE INITIATIVE III	CO	$1,000,000	$3,218,850	$0	$5,000	$3,223,850	$4,223,850	1,977
SOUTHCENTRAL WISCONSIN PRAIRIE POTHOLE INITIATIVE V	WI	$1,000,000	$4,477,920	$0	$31,000	$4,508,920	$5,508,920	3,312
SOUTHEAST WISCONSIN COASTAL HABITAT INITIATIVE, PHASE V	WI	$1,000,000	$3,082,988	$0	$12,000	$3,094,988	$4,094,988	1,836
SOUTHERN SAN JOAQUIN VALLEY WETLAND HABITAT PROJECT, PHASE I	CA	$1,000,000	$1,071,931	$0	$12,600	$1,084,531	$2,084,531	4,189

Table 3. U.S. Wetlands Conservation Standard Grants Proposals *(continued)*

Project Name	State Province	NAWCA Grant	Non-Fed Match	Non-Fed Non-Match	Federal Funds	Total Partners	Total Cost	Total Acres
ST. JOHNS RIVER HEADWATERS, PHASE II	FL	$1,000,000	$2,005,000	$0	$0	$2,005,000	$3,005,000	350
SUISUN MARSH MANAGED WETLAND ENHANCEMENT PROJECT, PHASE III	CA	$1,000,000	$1,005,884	$0	$0	$1,005,884	$2,005,884	10,860
TEXAS CHENIER PLAIN WETLAND REST & ENH OF PRIVATE & PUBLIC LANDS III	TX	$999,900	$2,127,773	$0	$0	$2,127,773	$3,127,673	1,525
UPPER IOWA PRAIRIE POTHOLE PARTNERSHIP, PHASE II	IA	$1,000,000	$2,005,000	$0	$20,000	$2,025,000	$3,025,000	762
VERMILION BAY COASTAL WETLANDS RESTORATION	LA	$1,000,000	$2,782,531	$0	$0	$2,782,531	$3,782,531	7,605
WEST PONTCHARTRAIN, MAUREPAS SWAMP IBA HABITAT CONSERVATION EFFORT	LA	$1,000,000	$2,215,000	$6,587,280	$0	$8,802,280	$9,802,280	1,914
WETLANDS REST & ENH OF PRIVATE & PUBLIC LANDS, TEXAS GULF COAST VIII	TX	$998,000	$1,496,609	$0	$100,000	$1,596,609	$2,594,609	3,025
WHITE AND CACHE RIVERS WETLANDS CONSERVATION PROJECT	AR	$985,000	$2,146,750	$0	$4,400	$2,151,150	$3,136,150	1,280
WINYAH BAY PROTECTION PROJECT: PHASE III	SC	$1,000,000	$12,305,078	$0	$0	$12,305,078	$13,305,078	2,166
Number of Projects: 50		$49,306,106	$141,932,510	$14,527,382	$7,478,761	$163,938,653	$213,244,759	235,356

Table 4. U.S. Wetlands Conservation Small Grant Proposals

Project Name	State Province	NAWCA Grant	Non-Fed Match	Non-Fed Non-Match	Federal Funds	Total Partners	Total Cost	Total Acres
ARKANSAS RIVER VALLEY WETLANDS RESTORATION PHASE I	AR	$75,000	$103,000	$0	$5,000	$108,000	$183,000	1,412
BALLARD COUNTY WILDLIFE MANAGEMENT AREA WETLAND ENHANCEMENT PROJECT	KY	$75,000	$277,900	$0	$0	$277,900	$352,900	238
BARN ISLAND WILDLIFE MANAGEMENT AREA EXPANSION PROJECT	CT	$75,000	$402,250	$1,335,250	$1,397,500	$3,135,000	$3,210,000	71
BLACKWATER POOLS 3 & 5 WETLAND RESTORATION	MD	$75,000	$126,240	$0	$5,000	$131,240	$206,240	141
BROUSSARD WETLANDS ENHANCEMENT	LA,TX	$75,000	$97,836	$0	$0	$97,836	$172,836	393
BUZZARDS BAY: MATTAPOISETT RIVER WETLANDS	MA	$75,000	$380,000	$0	$0	$380,000	$455,000	116
CENTRAL PENJAJAWOC PROPERTY ACQUISITION	ME	$75,000	$149,471	$0	$0	$149,471	$224,471	75
CHEHALIS WILDLIFE AREA EXPANSION	WA	$75,000	$92,000	$0	$100,000	$192,000	$267,000	76
COX HALL CREEK WETLAND RESTORATION	NJ	$75,000	$75,000	$0	$10,000	$85,000	$160,000	287
CRAZY WOMAN BISON RANCH CONSERVATION EASEMENT	MT	$75,000	$155,000	$0	$0	$155,000	$230,000	2,466
CROCKETT LAKE EAST WETLANDS	WA	$75,000	$150,000	$0	$262,500	$412,500	$487,500	138
DEWEES ISLAND OLD HOUSE LAGOON RESTORATION AND ENHANCEMENT	SC	$75,000	$92,322	$1,337	$1,478	$95,137	$170,137	120
EPHRATA LAKE ACQUISITION	WA	$75,000	$75,000	$0	$100,000	$175,000	$250,000	560
FENMONT WMA	MN	$75,000	$162,566	$0	$0	$162,566	$237,566	40
GCJV MOTTLED DUCK CONSERVATION PLAN, PHASE IV	TX	$32,000	$87,000	$0	$0	$87,000	$119,000	2,250
GOODYEAR DUCK CLUB ENHANCEMENT PROJECT	CA	$75,000	$75,000	$0	$0	$75,000	$150,000	340
GRASSLANDS WETLAND ENHANCEMENT	CA	$75,000	$151,016	$0	$0	$151,016	$226,016	920
GRASSLANDS WETLAND RESTORATION AND UPLAND ENHANCEMENT PROJECT	CA	$75,000	$77,960	$0	$0	$77,960	$152,960	240
GREAT HEATH ECOLOGICAL RESERVE EXPANSION PROJECT	ME	$59,500	$105,500	$0	$1,000	$106,500	$166,000	366
HUNTER COVE, RANGELEY LAKE	ME	$75,000	$1,802,559	$0	$0	$1,802,559	$1,877,559	209
MADRENA WMA ADDITION	MN	$75,000	$277,000	$0	$0	$277,000	$352,000	160
MARSH ROAD ACQ AND RESTORATION OF THE LOWER WOLF RIVER BOTTOM WILDLIFE AREA	WI	$52,000	$98,700	$0	$0	$98,700	$150,700	45
MASON BAY COASTAL CONSERVATION AREA, PHASE III, UPPER WHITE CREEK SALT MARSH	ME	$75,000	$80,500	$0	$3,000	$83,500	$158,500	30
MEADOW VALLEY FLOWAGE WETLAND ENHANCEMENT PROJECT, PHASE II	WI	$75,000	$80,708	$0	$0	$80,708	$155,708	655
NORTHWEST WISCONSIN WETLAND & GRASSLAND PROGRAM, PHASE II	WI	$68,646	$68,646	$0	$0	$68,646	$137,292	210
OCEAN POINT PRESERVE PROJECT	ME	$75,000	$255,000	$130,455	$3,000	$388,455	$463,455	25
PAWTUCKAWAY RIVER GREENWAY, PHASE II	NH	$41,500	$41,500	$25,000	$247,000	$313,500	$355,000	175

Table 4. U.S. Wetlands Conservation Small Grant Proposals *(continued)*

Project Name	State Province	NAWCA Grant	Non-Fed Match	Non-Fed Non-Match	Federal Funds	Total Partners	Total Cost	Total Acres
PURDY RANCH PLAYA AND NATIVE GRASSLANDS CONSERVATION PROJECT	CO	$75,000	$1,794,500	$0	$0	$1,794,500	$1,869,500	8,684
PURPLE SAGE RANCH OXBOW WETLAND RESTORATION	WY	$50,000	$178,250	$0	$72,708	$250,958	$300,958	89
RASLYNN WATERFOWL COMPLEX ADDITION	MN	$75,000	$211,600	$0	$0	$211,600	$286,600	88
RICH VALLEY WATERFOWL COMPLEX ADDITION	MN	$75,000	$186,000	$0	$0	$186,000	$261,000	80
RIPARIAN & WETLANDS RESTORATION IN THE JEMEZ MOUNTAINS	NM	$75,000	$257,042	$0	$250,310	$507,352	$582,352	220
SANGAMON BAY & TREADWAY LAKE PERMANENT CONSERVATION EASEMENTS	IL	$75,000	$138,100	$0	$0	$138,100	$213,100	658
SCHULTZ LAKE WETLAND ENHANCEMENT	MI	$39,148	$39,326	$0	$0	$39,326	$78,474	38
SHEFFIELD, EGREMONT AGRICULTURAL, ECOLOGICAL & SCENIC CORRIDOR, WETLAND HAB	MA	$75,000	$250,000	$3,670,000	$0	$3,920,000	$3,995,000	29
SLATE CREEK WETLANDS	KS	$75,000	$307,218	$7,230	$0	$314,448	$389,448	173
SMELT BROOK CONSERVATION AREA	ME	$75,000	$515,000	$69,750	$0	$584,750	$659,750	30
THEODORE ROOSEVELT NWR COMPLEX, WETLAND HAB REST & AG RUN-OFF ABATEMENT	MS	$75,000	$96,492	$0	$9,530	$106,022	$181,022	450
UPPER GREAT MARSH TIDAL MARSH RESTORATION	MA	$75,000	$134,492	$0	$7,500	$141,992	$216,992	450
UPPER WOLF RIVER, SPINOLO TRACT ACQUISITION	TN	$75,000	$170,850	$0	$0	$170,850	$245,850	154
WET MEADOW RESTORATION AT HENNEPIN & HOPPER LAKES	IL	$75,000	$152,400	$0	$0	$152,400	$227,400	120
WHITE RIVER VALLEY IRRIGATED RANCHLANDS CONSERVATION PROJECT	CO	$75,000	$2,416,000	$0	$628,000	$3,044,000	$3,119,000	1,373
WILD WINGS WMA ADDITION	MN	$75,000	$99,866	$0	$0	$99,866	$174,866	50
WISCONSIN PRIVATE LAND WETLAND RESTORATION PROJECT	WI	$50,000	$60,500	$0	$5,000	$65,500	$115,500	425
WOLF LAKE WPA	MN	$75,000	$233,875	$0	$0	$233,875	$308,875	148
Number of Projects: 45		$3,167,794	$12,781,185	$5,239,022	$3,108,526	$21,128,732	$24,296,526	25,017

Table 5. Canadian Wetlands Conservation Proposals

Project Name	State Province	NAWCA Grant	Non-Fed Match	Non-Fed Non-Match	Federal Funds	Total Partners	Total Cost	Total Acres
BRITISH COLUMBIA PACIFIC COAST & CANADIAN INTERMOUNTAIN CONS PROG 2011-3	AB,BC	$2,154,344	$2,154,344	$200,000	$0	$2,354,344	$4,508,688	2,204
CANADIAN PRAIRIE/PARKLAND AND WESTERN BOREAL HABITAT PROGRAM 2011-3	AB,BC,MB, NT,SK,YT	$15,726,709	$15,726,709	$5,581,000	$138,000	$21,445,709	$37,172,418	122,951
DUC / EASTERN HABITAT JOINT VENTURE WETLANDS CONSERVATION 2011-3	NB,NF,NS,ON, PE,QC	$3,662,424	$3,662,424	$1,625,338	$0	$5,287,762	$8,950,186	4,931
NCC BRITISH COLUMBIA: CIJV & PCJV WETLAND-ASSOC MIG BIRD HABITAT CONS 2011-3	BC	$515,663	$515,663	$1,417,317	$0	$1,932,980	$2,448,643	239
NCC QUEBEC & ATLANTIC: PROTECTING WETLAND & UPLAND HABITAT 2011-3, EHJV	NB,NF,NS,PE,QC	$843,812	$843,812	$755,376	$0	$1,599,188	$2,443,000	2,200
POTHOLES PLUS PROGRAM	MB	$656,298	$656,298	$617,404	$0	$1,273,702	$1,930,000	7,200
Number of Projects: 6		$23,559,250	$23,559,250	$10,196,435	$138,000	$33,893,685	$57,452,935	139,725

Table 6. Mexican Wetlands Conservation Proposals

Project Name	State Province	NAWCA Grant	Non-Fed Match	Non-Fed Non-Match	Federal Funds	Total Partners	Total Cost	Total Acres
CONS. OF THE PACIFIC BRANT WINTERING HABITAT IN THE VIZCAINO WETLANDS	BCS	$250,000	$1,675,144	$0	$0	$1,675,144	$1,925,144	226,314
CONSERVATION OF PRIORITY WETLANDS IN THE YUCATAN PENINSULA, PHASE 2	Q.ROO,YUC	$700,000	$892,580	$0	$0	$892,580	$1,592,580	988
HABITAT PROTECTION FOR MIG. BIRDS IN BAHIA MAGDALENA-ALMEJAS WETLAND COMPLEX II	BCS	$450,829	$1,292,636	$0	$0	$1,292,636	$1,743,465	1,134
INVENTORY & CLASSIFICATION OF CRITICAL WETLANDS IN MEXICO, PHASE VI: N. HIGHLAND	CHIH,COAH,DGO, NL,SIN,SLP,SON, TAMPS,ZAC	$352,032	$391,120	$0	$0	$391,120	$743,152	0
PROTECTION AND MANAGEMENT OF LAGUNA BABICORA, CHIHUAHUA PHASE II	CHIH	$285,064	$393,005	$0	$0	$393,005	$678,069	35,582
PROTECTION AND RESTORATION ON THE RIO BRAVO DELTA: LAGUNA MADRE PHASE II	TAMPS	$493,165	$14,141,600	$0	$0	$14,141,600	$14,634,765	12,350
REST. & CREATION OF FRESH WATER WETLANDS ADJACENT TO LAGUNA MADRE	TAMPS	$179,156	$195,382	$0	$0	$195,382	$374,538	721
REST. AND ALTERNATIVES FOR THE SUSTAINABILITY OF THE ALVARADO LAGOON SYSTEM	VER	$259,978	$417,343	$0	$0	$417,343	$677,321	124
Number of Projects: 8		$2,970,224	$19,398,810	$0	$0	$19,398,810	$22,369,034	277,213

Membership of the Migratory Bird Conservation Commission

Fiscal Year	Secretary of the Interior[1]	Secretary of Agriculture[2]	Secretary of Commerce[3]	Secretary of Transportation[4]	Administrator of EPA[5]	Members on Part of the Senate		Members on Part of the House		Secretary to the Commission
1929	Roy L. Wilbur	Arthur M. Hyde	Robert P. Lamont			Harry B. Hawes	Peter Norbeck	Sam D. McReynolds	Ernest R. Ackerman	Rudolph Dieffenbach
1930										
1931										
1932									August H. Anderson	
1933	Harold L. Ickes	Henry A. Wallace	Daniel C. Roper			Key Pittman			Roy O. Woodruff	
1934									Chester C. Bolton	
1935										
1936										
1937							Charles L McNary		James Wolfenden	
1938										
1939			Harry L. Hopkins							
1940						George L Radcliffe		John J. Cochran		
1941		Claude R Wickard	Jessie H. Jones							
1942										
1943										
1944							Vacant		Walter E. Brehm	
1945		Clinton P. Anderson	Henry A. Wallace				C. Wayland Brooks			
1946	Julius A Krug									
1947			W. Averell Harriman			A. Willis Robertson		Frank M. Karsten		Arthur A. Riemer
1948		Charles F. Brannon	Charles W. Sawyer							
1949							Raymond E. Baldwin			
1950	Oscar L. Chapman						Vacant			
1951							John W. Bricker			
1952									August H. Anderson	
1953	Douglas McKay	Ezra Taft Benson	Sinclair Weeks							
1954										
1955										
1956	Fred A. Seaton					Thomas C. Hennings, Jr.				
1957			Lewis L. Strauss							Albert J. Rissman
1958			Frederick H. Mueller							
1959							Roman L. Hruska		Leon H. Gavin	
1960										
1961	Stewart L. Udall	Orville L. Freeman	Luther H. Hodges			Lee Metcalf				
1962										
1963										
1964									George A. Gooding	
1965			John T. Connor						Silvio O. Conte	F.G. Spoden Jr.
1966										
1967			Alexander B. Trowbridge							
1968				Alan S. Boyd						
1969	Walter J. Hickel	Clifford M. Hardin		John A. Volpe		Henry L. Bellman		John D. Dingell		

Fiscal Year	Secretary of the Interior[1]	Secretary of Agriculture[2]	Secretary of Commerce[3]	Secretary of Transportation[4]	Administrator of EPA[5]	Members on Part of the Senate	Members on Part of the House	Secretary to the Commission
1970						Joseph D. Tydings		
1971	Rogers C.B. Morton					Lee Metcalf		Walter R. McAllister
1972		Earl L. Butz						
1973				Claude S. Brinegar				
1974								
1975	Stanley Hathaway			William T. Coleman		Quentin N. Burdick		
1976	Thomas S. Kleppe							
1977	Cecil D. Andrus	Bob Bergland		Brook Adams		Royd K. Haskell		
1978								
1979				Neil Goldschmidt		David H. Pryor		
1980								
1981	James G. Watt	James R. Block		Drew Lewis		Thad Cochran		
1982								
1983				Elizabeth H. Dole				
1984	William P. Clark							
1985	Donald Hodel							
1986		Richard Lyng						
1987				James Burnley IV				
1988								
1989	Manuel Lujan Jr.	Clayton Yeutter		Samuel K. Skinner				
1990							Richard T. Schulze	
1991		Edward R. Madigan			William K. Reilly			
1992								Geoffrey L. Haskett
1993	Bruce Babbitt	Mike Espy			Carol M. Browner		Curt Weldon	
1994								
1995		Daniel R. Glickman						Jeffery M. Donahue
1996						John B. Breaux		William F. Hartwig
1997								
1998								
1999								
2000								
2001	Gale Norton	Ann M. Veneman			Christine Todd-Whitman			
2002								
2003					Michael O. Leavitt			A. Eric Alvarez
2004								
2005		Mike Johanns			Stephen L. Johnson	Blanche L. Lincoln		
2006	Dirk Kempthorne							
2007							Wayne T. Gilchrest	
2008		Edward Schafer						
2009	Kenneth L. Salazar	Thomas J. Vilsack			Lisa P. Jackson		Robert J. Wittman	
2010								
2011						Mark Pryor		

1. Chairman, 1940 to date
2. Chairman, 1929 to 1939
3. Member, 1929 to March 1, 1968
4. Member, March 2, 1968 to December 12, 1989
5. Member, December 13, 1989 to date

www.ingramcontent.com/pod-product-compliance
Lightning Source LLC
Chambersburg PA
CBHW052020280526
45793CB00005B/1057